"This book is filled with so much wisdom that it should be required reading for all those who aspire to be leaders. I would pair it with Jim Collins' *Good to Great* as the two most important guides for leaders today."

Jon Masters, Chairman, Masters Governance Consulting

"The great stories in this book demonstrate how the best leaders focus clearly on practical ways of building those bonds of loyalty between the company and its people that prove so critical in turbulent times."

**Lynn Casey, Chairman and Chief Executive Officer,
Padilla Speer Beardsley, Inc.**

"Goman has captured the key elements that we are facing in our changing world. Those who keep up will do very well and others, I'm afraid, will be passed over."

Charles Lynch, Chairman, Market Value Partners Co.

"Using an intriguing combination of stories, interviews, and structure, Carol Kinsey Goman has written a 'must read' for anyone involved in leadership. This book is for people who have arrived as well as those just starting out."

**Robert L. Dilenschneider, Chief Executive Officer,
The Dilenschneider Group**

"Change's best friend is this book. Carol Kinsey Goman has produced a highly enjoyable and informative book about organizational change, loyalty, and the challenges of transformation."

Lee Hornick, Program Director, The Conference Board

"*This Isn't the Company I Joined* is a creative and provocative guide to effective change leadership. Goman's insights will help leaders at all levels of an organization survive — even thrive — in a constantly changing business environment."

Marci Rubin, Deputy General Counsel, Wells Fargo Bank

"The stories and success models shown here will help leaders break their paradigm paralysis. They affirm change and prove it can be exciting, even joyous."

**Susan Gordon, Director, Center for Professional
Development, Belmont University**

"World events and business climates are changing at a staggering pace. This book hits the mark with practical up-to-date suggestions for success that are well suited for employer and employee alike."

John W. Adams, International Financial Consultant

"This Isn't the Company I Joined"

HOW TO LEAD IN A BUSINESS TURNED UPSIDE DOWN

CAROL KINSEY GOMAN

ISBN: 0-9625435-2-7
Printed in the United States of America

Published by KCS Publishing
P.O. Box 8255
Berkeley, CA 94707
(510) 526-1727
Fax: (510) 524-9577
E-mail: cgoman@ckg.com
Web: www.CKG.com

This publication is designed to provide accurate and authoritative information in regard to the subject matter covered. It is sold with the understanding that the publisher is not engaged in rendering legal, accounting, or other professional services. If legal advice or other expert assistance is required, the services of a competent person should be sought.

**Publisher's Cataloging-in-Publication
(Provided by Quality Books, Inc.)**
Goman, Carol Kinsey.
    "This isn't the company I joined" : how to lead in a business turned upside down / Carol Kinsey Goman.
    p. cm.
    Includes index.
    ISBN 0-9625435-2-7

    1. Organizational change. 2. Corporate reorganizations. 3. Organizational behavior.
I. Title.
    HD58.8.G653 2004   658.4'063
                        QBI03-200927

CONTENTS

INTRODUCTION

THE TRUTH SLOWLY DAWNS on the business managers assembled before me. "How many of you have noticed," I ask them, "that the company you are working for today is not the one you joined a year or a month or even a week ago?" Hands start to rise. They're catching on, beginning to grasp that even if they had started their jobs only yesterday, something about the organization they joined has already changed.

It takes several minutes probing before I've collected enough information to measure the audience's exact mood about this situation. I ask them to describe the kinds and the quality of internal changes they are facing. I ask them to comment on the impact of these changes on office morale and individual performance. Naturally, exact responses differ with each company, but from the hundreds of presentations I've given to corporate and association clients on the human side of organizational change, one common emotional theme seems always to emerge: Anxiety. The sense, spreading from worker to worker like a kind of contagious confusion, is that the organization they thought they joined has been turned upside-down — and that they have no idea what to do about it!

As corporate policy-makers are asked to respond ever more quickly to the pressures and opportunities of today's rapidly changing business environment, so more workers find themselves being thrust into unfamiliar roles that involve responsibilities they'd never agreed to undertake and the exercise of skills they'd never claimed to possess. People who've always worked solo in the past are bustled into teams and told to "collaborate."

Technical experts are suddenly instructed to brush up their "people skills," while "people" workers with no technical background are warned to stay abreast of technical trends or risk becoming obsolete. Employees at all levels are ordered to re-engineer their jobs to meet the latest company challenges, having no clear understanding of exactly what those challenges are and fearing that in trying to comply they may unwittingly make themselves redundant. Job security is gone. Stress levels and work loads are rising. Everything is changing rapidly, dramatically, and irrevocably. No wonder employees feel confused.

Except that change itself isn't the problem from the employee's perspective. The problem for the employee is leadership. Workers are resilient, resourceful people. They can live with transformation. They can adapt and even thrive on change — if their leaders make change comprehensible to them; if they show their team that "upside-down" is in fact a positive, exciting place to be — a place where they can grow, learn, expand their talents, explore their potentials, increase their earning power, energize themselves for the future and above all move constructively with the changing times. Because change, as we have all come to learn, is what defines the 21st century business dynamic. Today "upside-down" is not only a good place to be, it's the ONLY place to be.

Convincing a skeptical, resistant workforce of this, however, will require the creation and application of new organizational and leadership models. Not an easy task when you remember that the new models will have to be tested on the front line as they evolve. As one Silicon Valley leader put it: "It took 400 years for business organizations to figure out how to operate successfully in the Industrial Age. We are only starting to understand how to operate in the Information Age. We're at the beginning of an experiment."

INTENDED AUDIENCE FOR
"THIS ISN'T THE COMPANY I JOINED"

MODERN LEADERS MUST WORK HARDER and smarter than ever to keep their organizations productive and competitive. The processes they use to manage change must keep pace with trends in the ways their employees think and act. This new edition provides renewed perspective on the fragile art of employee communication and motivation. It's written primarily for leaders who face employee resistance to the accelerating change that defines the Information Age. I use a broad definition of the term "leader" to include not just senior executives like CEOs, business unit presidents, and function heads, but also managers throughout the ranks who lead departments, work teams, and staffs. This book is also intended for the professionals who assist executives and managers to develop motivational strategies for a changing workplace. These include corporate communications, human resources, and strategic planning personnel. Finally, this book is valuable to any individual employee who wants to benefit from a deeper understanding of new business realities and changing strategies for success.

ACKNOWLEDGMENTS

DURING THE RESEARCH for this book, I received assistance from countless individuals and organizations. Members of the Council of Communication Management deserve special mention for their unfailing generosity and support. I'd also like to express my appreciation to the following organizations for giving me access to their leaders and for sharing their collaboration and change-management "success stories."

Adelphia Communications
Agilent Technologies
Allstate Insurance
AlixPartners
BEA Systems
Buckman Laboratories
Caterpillar
Cisco Systems
Federal Express
Fluor
J.M. Huber Corporation
John Deere
Ketchum
Leap Wireless
Lockheed Martin
Nordstrom
Northrop Grumman
Pacific Northwest National Laboratory
Planned Parenthood Federation
Playboy Enterprises

Reell Precision Manufacturing
Royal Bank of Canada
Sankyo Pharma
SC Johnson Wax
Springfield Remanufacturing
The Dilenschneider Group
The Ritz-Carlton Hotel Company
Vitesse
Washington Mutual
William Blair & Company

To George Kimball, who edited this book, I owe a deep debt of gratitude. Ours is a true collaboration and his contribution is enormous.

To Richard Truitt, who guided me in this project, I extend my heartfelt thanks for his savvy, his creativity and his good common sense.

And to my husband, Ray K. Goman, who loved and tolerated me throughout the whole process, I can finally answer "Yes!" to his question: "Are you ever coming out of your office?"

THE AUTHOR

CAROL KINSEY GOMAN knows that a business turned upside-down can be a stimulating workplace for employees, particularly in a well-managed firm. It can serve to spread knowledge readily through the organization, award authority to workers and rebuild their relationships with management.

But that's not usually the way it works, she says. The process of change and the new systems it brings can be traumatic and even terrifying for employees who are not properly prepared for a devastating market reversal or the downsizing of a department.

Because organizational change can take place both in bad times and in good, as in the case of rebuilding a successful company to assure it remains competitive, Carol Goman sees the shaking and reshaping of organizations as a trend that will be with us for some time.

For this reason, she says, change managers need access to examples of leadership and models of organizational structure that will help them bring employees together and solve ongoing problems collectively. In several of her books, and in seminars that she presents regularly around the world, she shows how knowledge-sharing helps facilitate change, and how worker-sensitive management stimulates knowledge-sharing.

Kinsey Consulting Services, her firm, has served more than 90 organizations in 19 countries — corporate giants, major non-profits, and government agencies. Clients include Consolidated Edison, 3M, Bayer Pharmaceutical, BP, PepsiCo, the American Institute of Banking, Hewlett-Packard and the Office of the

Comptroller of the Currency. Information about the company can be found at www.CKG.com.

Before she founded the firm, she was a therapist in private practice specializing in short-term therapy for behavioral change. She lives in Berkeley, California.

CHAPTER 1

A CHANGING REALITY

"How can I play the game when the rules keep changing?"

FIVE FUNDAMENTAL EVENTS have created the new business dynamic that all leaders and staff must come to terms with today:

1. The shift from domestic to global competition.
2. The shift from manpower to techno-power.
3. The shift from company-led to consumer-driven market forces.
4. The shift from the Industrial Economy to the Knowledge Economy.
5. The demographic shift of the workforce and the resulting transformation of employer/employee relations.

These five forces are the defining events of the post-Industrial age, and together they have turned a once predictable landscape into a place where constant instability is the only "certainty" that can be relied upon.

1. GLOBALIZATION

> "For all practical purposes, all business today is global.
> Those individual businesses, firms, industries,
> and whole societies that clearly understand
> the new rules of doing business in a world economy
> will prosper; those that do not will perish."
> **Ira Mitroff, Professor,**
> **University of Southern California**

Prior to World War II, the number of American firms involved in foreign investment was relatively small. Even after the war, most United States business activity remained centered on its domestic markets — markets that continued to provide adequate scope for growth and a natural competitive monopoly. Foreign imports were insignificant through the 1950s, and the products America exported were the same products it sold at home — shipped abroad without alteration or sensitivity to cultural differences.

Then in the 1960s, this period of economic and cultural isolationism ended as (a) relaxed tariff policies allowed cheaper foreign imports to compete seriously with domestic goods in a rapidly expanding consumer economy, and (b) OPEC, with its new-found petro-power, began forcing American industry and America's drivers into a painful readjustment of their thinking about fuel costs. At the same time, America's cultural horizons began to broaden. Television brought the Vietnam war into the nation's living rooms — often on sets made by Vietnam's neighbors — and U.S. citizens started traveling abroad in large numbers for the first time in the country's history. By the 1980s, with the birth of the Asian Tigers and the opening of lucrative new markets in Europe, the Middle East and Africa, American business suddenly realized that it had some serious catching up to do in the areas of product design, quality, marketing, and overseas service if it wanted to compete successfully with its more experienced foreign opposition in the new global arena. Today, all aspects of business have become internationalized. The easy movement of money and people across borders, the creation of multi-national alliances and strategies, the revolution in information technology and the convergence of foreign cultures and markets have combined to turn the world into one huge shopping mall.

In the U.S., Europe and Asia, there have been huge increases in foreign investment over the past two decades. In the late 1980s, multinationals greatly stepped up their efforts to buy or build manufacturing and sales facilities in foreign target markets. By 2000, foreign firms, excluding banks, employed 6.4 million U.S. workers with a payroll of some $330 billion, according to the Commerce Department.

But globalization isn't a one-way street. Overseas goods, services, ideas and personnel are pouring into America just as quickly as they are being shipped out. Even small businesses now compete with and have access to products, labor, and new marketing techniques from all over the world. Today, component parts of well over half of the products built in the United States originate in other countries. Quality control and new product design, once domestically determined, now meet international standards as a matter of course. Competitors are no longer located just down the block. They are based in Malaysia and Chile and Finland and South Africa.

The same holds true for workforces. Employee pools, once thought of as geographically static, now migrate across international borders as easily as cars or computer chips. Companies can locate — or relocate — where the tax laws are most advantageous and where skilled, cost-effective labor is most readily available. Workloads can be spread over several time zones to cut production costs and facilitate delivery schedules. Individual technicians can go wherever their expertise is needed. Jobs can move to wherever talent resides. According to Forbes.com, analysts predict that by 2015, more than 3 million white-collar jobs in the U.S. will be outsourced to other countries.

Remember, however, that globalization has been an executive-led phenomenon. The workforce played no direct role in its development, and most employees will have little understanding of its dynamics. Because this lack of understanding can lead to confusion and even a collapse of commitment, it is the leader's job to make sure that people throughout the organization are fully informed about the company's global future and about how each employee fits personally into that future.

Here are some concrete strategies to help you accomplish that aim:

- Communicate your global mission and goals so that employees get used to thinking of the organization in an international context: Announce your international standings and revenues, talk about global challenges and opportunities region by region, and explain how your various overseas locations support one another and contribute to corporate objectives.
- Include news of international activity in all organizational communications — from employee newsletters and corporate intranets to speeches from senior management. Discuss the ways in which trends, events, treaties, currency fluctuations, and laws around the world impact the organization.
- Offer courses in how to do business in other countries. Invite all employees to attend.
- Encourage employees to learn a second (or third) language. Acknowledge and reward them for acquiring these additional language skills.
- At company meetings, bring in speakers from other global organizations and ask for their stories about the impact of globalization on their businesses. Invite overseas managers from your organization to make presentations

in the United States. Encourage repatriated employees to describe their experiences abroad.

• Review organizational policies on recruiting, training and relocating employees to make sure there is a global emphasis.

• Reward employees with trips abroad to attend international conferences, to visit your facility in another country, or to meet with customers in other countries.

2. THE TECHNOLOGICAL REVOLUTION

> "The Third Wave sector includes not only high-flying computer and electronic firms or biotech start-ups. It embraces advanced information-driven manufacturing in every industry. It includes the increasingly data-drenched services — finance, software, entertainment, the media, advanced communications, medical services, consulting, training, and education — in short, all the industries based on mind-work rather than muscle-work."
> **Alvin Toffler**

Advances in technology drive change throughout organizations, enabling them to improve their business processes by replacing routine activities with information systems and robotics. Instant electronic transmission makes it possible to move data entry jobs to any location on the globe. Advances in electronic networking permit the redistribution of power in organizations, making it feasible for employees to skip levels in the chain of command, providing senior executives with direct access to employee feedback on performance and organizational issues, and making workers at remote sites feel that they are part of the team.

Technology is also opening up a world of true employee participation in business decision-making. Intranet systems allow organizations to capture and share knowledge throughout the organization, to exchange best practices and good ideas company-wide, and to reinforce the corporate culture. P2P (peer-to-peer) computing, where computers communicate directly with each other, gives people in different departments and different regions of the world instant access to one another.

Technology is providing employees with direct access to information necessary for business decisions. This transfer of knowledge directly to workers has made possible — and inevitable — many of the changes in the organizational structure of the corporation, and has been one of the major forces behind increasing employee empowerment.

That is the good news. The downside, of course, is the loss of jobs. Automated teller machines, robots, and electronic voice mail replace human bank tellers, assembly-line workers, and telephone operators who all used to collect paychecks and are now collecting unemployment.

In their book, *The One to One Future,* authors Don Peppers and Martha Rogers use this example to illustrate how technology affects workers: "When one of the first steam shovels went into use, a story is told about the union boss who confronted the construction company president with a demand that he stop using the machine as it would put several dozen laborers out of work. He wanted the construction company to agree to continue using work crews with shovels. In response, the executive offered to eliminate the shovel, too, and replace it with a teaspoon — to provide even more jobs."

3. CUSTOMER POWER

"In India, we refer to customers as 'Emperors of Choice.'"
K.M. Mammen,
Vice Chairman and Managing Director, M.R.F. Ltd.

Consumers around the globe are becoming relentless in their demands for quality, service, customization, convenience, speed and competitive pricing. And with global competition and the new technologies providing customers greater choice about when, how, and where they will receive goods and services, they have, in effect, become *the* determining factor in the success or failure of most organizations. We are selling products and services to an increasingly informed and sophisticated consumer today; consumers are no longer prepared to pay inflated prices for less than ideal goods because of their brand names or because no equivalent product is available. Today there is *always* an equivalent product available somewhere in the world — and a customer ready to defect to the competition if your version doesn't come up to their standards.

When Armstrong International Corporation first started selling steam traps in Japan, they received complaints about how the traps looked. Appearance doesn't affect performance, of course, but since the Japanese expected no nicks, blemishes or color distortions on their products, Armstrong immediately changed to a high-pigment paint that produced a richer-looking paint job and began shipping the traps in individual packing so they didn't bump one another in transit. The Japanese renewed the contract and Armstrong saved a valuable customer at a cost of only a few cents per unit.

Marketing strategies, as well as quality considerations, have undergone similar transformations in ways ranging from packaging and logo design to television and print media advertising techniques. How products and services are sold to customers today has become just as important as the products themselves. In the retail sector, leaders look for new ways to reach the new customer, targeting in particular the growing number of dual-income consumers who have more to spend but less time to shop. It is now commonplace to see 24-hour grocery stores, pharmacies and laundromats. Gas stations sell food, supermarkets offer banking and pharmacy services, and banks let you do it all online. In fact, one of the biggest trends is the increase in access of direct sales into the home and business markets through catalogues, home shopping channels on televisions, and the internet.

When customers link with technology, they create a force which businesses have never encountered before. Old philosophy about customer service stated that when someone had a bad experience with a product, they told seven other people. With the help of technology, this number can jump dramatically.

Take Tom and Shane, for instance, a couple of internet consultants from Seattle who had made guaranteed reservations at the Doubletree Suites Hotel in Houston. When they arrived at 2 a.m., the night clerk told them there were no rooms, and, after some unpleasant remarks, made accommodations for them at what the pair felt was a less-than-adequate hotel. Rather than confiding their discontent to a few friends, Tom and Shane used the internet to post a PowerPoint presentation about their experience, which was ultimately viewed by approximately 40,000 people.

What did this mean to the Doubletree?

- The public outcry led the Doubletree manager to call and apologize to Tom and Shane.
- The Doubletree got so many phone calls about the presentation that it began to affect their ability to handle day-to-day business.
- The result: Doubletree radically overhauled its training policies.

The new standard of excellence for all organizations today is meeting, or exceeding, customer expectations. To this end, companies are organizing around personnel with direct customer contact, encouraging customer critique, listening to what they say, empowering employees to satisfy customer demands on the spot whenever possible, and involving customers in the process of developing new products and services.

As a leader, you promote the critical employee/customer relationship when you:

- Invite a panel of customers to address employees and have the customers say what they like and don't like about your company's products/services.
- Send employees to your customer's place of business and let workers personally see the business challenges and problems that the customer faces.
- Use customer questionnaires and publish the results — both positive and negative. And when the negative comments point to a specific problem, create an employee-customer task-force to investigate and solve it.
- Invite customers to attend strategy sessions and product development meetings.
- Publish every letter of praise or complaint that comes from customers.
- Make "heroes" out of workers who solve customers' problem in creative ways, by telling their stories in your speeches and other corporate communications.
- Create an "idea campaign" around the question *"How can we surprise and delight the customer?"*
- Send employees to trade shows that are also attended by customers.

4. THE KNOWLEDGE ECONOMY

> "With everything else dropping out of the competitive equation, knowledge has become the only source of long-run sustainable competitive advantage."
> **Lester Thurow,**
> **Professor of Management and Economics, MIT**

The shift from industrial to knowledge-based organizations has occurred with extraordinary swiftness in this country, and its impact upon our thinking about work and the workplace has been as profound as that experienced in the 19th century when America shifted from being an agricultural nation to an industrial one. In fact, the challenges of the knowledge economy are impacting every aspect of the workplace. Only a generation ago, trained technical workers were a relative rarity in this country. Now they comprise nearly a quarter of the total American workforce.

The most highly skilled, the so-called "gold collar workers," are engaged in steadily more specialized activities, while the tasks demanding less rigorous training (technical and legal research, lab analysis, computer programming and the like) are being handed over to a growing body of "paraprofessional" support workers whose roles in today's service/information world equate roughly to those carried out by skilled mechanics and quality control engineers in the Industrial Age. Specialized sub-contractors in a variety of technical fields are also proliferating as large professional organizations like hospitals, consulting companies, law firms, multi-national publishers and media conglomerates find that detailed work once done in-house can be done faster, more cost-effectively and often better by independent specialists.

But knowledge work extends well beyond the limits of technology specialists. In the Industrial Age, companies squandered immense amounts of human potential on mindless, repetitive tasks and meaningless paper work. It never occurred to leaders in those days that their assembly-line workers had the know-how to go home and rebuild entire car engines, that their "lowly cashiers" easily negotiated complicated bank loans for their families, or that their "pretty little stenographers" were perfectly capable of chairing PTA meetings, managing household budgets, organizing charity drives, sitting on hospital committees or running complex volunteer organizations in their spare time. In the post-Industrial Information Age, no company can afford to waste human capital so rashly. Every talent, every idea, every skill is needed urgently if companies are to survive in the new global economy. The potential of the workforce *really is* the company's greatest asset today.

Chaparral Steel, a mill in Midlothian, Texas, that produces new products from recycled steel, is an example of an industrial firm that makes creating and using knowledge a part of everyone's job. Even the first-line associate is expected to work on production experiments, to identify new product offerings, and to propose new process designs. Chaparral's culture is nonhierarchical and workers are trusted to be highly productive without monitoring.

Lord Rees-Mogg, former editor of the *Times of London* said, "In the future, more businesses will be based on intangibles than on tangibles." And with that shift comes a whole new list of priorities and challenges in the management and development of a workforce:

- The new business fundamentals include an increasing focus on knowledge, trust, relationships, communities, and networks.
- Leadership styles change as upper executives learn to consult skilled workers on a wide variety of issues. Employees gain new power with the authority to make decisions based on the data they develop.
- Collaboration and teamwork become essential as members from research and development, marketing and manufacturing work together on all stages of product development.
- Both managers and workers now accept the necessity for lifelong learning. So much so that continuous professional development actually becomes a term of employment. Even small companies, faced with the reality of accelerating knowledge obsolescence, have come to accept employee training as an investment rather than an expense.

5. THE CHANGING WORKFORCE

"Why can't they be like we were ... perfect in every way?"
From the song, *Kids*, from the show "Bye Bye Birdie"

In fundamentally important ways, the workforces you are hiring today are not the workforces you would have been hiring only a generation ago. The differences in demographic makeup, social conditions, life experience and individual expectations have already become enormous. Of the changing realities being examined in this chapter, the transformation of the workforce is the one that impacts most critically upon corporate survival in the new business age.

In workplaces of all types, from high-tech cubicles to established factories to government offices, new technologies and new ways of organizing work are eroding old hierarchies. Experience may still carry some weight, but organizations sometimes favor those younger and more technologically savvy — often creating the potential for friction between the age groups.

At present, the American workforce is still dominated statistically by Baby Boomers — 76 million men and women born between 1946 and 1964 who began taking over the job market in the 1960s, survived two serious recessions in the 70s and 80s, and came out the other side. Now a new generation of workers — Generation X — is feeding into the equation, 44 million people born between 1965 and 1983. And following them, the so-called Millennial Generation, is already making its demands known: more values and meaning incorporated into company culture, more flexibility than even Generation X wants, plus more information, more quickly. These are all needs that companies are going to have to satisfy if they want to attract and retain the best employees.

The War for Talent

While the most tangible magnet for talent in the dot.com economy was money, the most important lessons emerged from the changing culture and work environment it engendered. Dot.com competition forced formerly stodgy institutions to be more responsive to the changing needs of their employees, and those lessons should be remembered as we look to the future. The war for talent isn't over. Understanding and meeting the demands of your best and brightest will play an increasingly important role in reaching your business objectives. In the future, top talent in all industries will increasingly demand that information is shared and organized in ways that help them work smarter and faster, and that they are given the tools, jobs, projects, and training that best develop their skills and talents.

It's amazing how employees want to stay with an organization whose culture reflects their own values — and how quickly they feel out of place when there is a cultural misalignment. That's why smart companies take the time to identify new employees' skills, talents, ideal work environments, and personal values, and then integrate those new hires into the culture as quickly as possible. The sooner employees can get to work doing what they're good at, in an environment that suits their personal work style, the more positive they feel about themselves and the organization.

Today's top talent is self-reliant and confident; it is also poised to seek new jobs if its needs aren't met. In order to keep top performers from leaving the company as soon as other opportunities arise, key players need to be identified and continually "re-recruited." The process of re-recruiting top talent manifests as an ongoing conversation between managers and their most valuable employees, and it begins with bosses knowing the answers to questions like these:

- Why do your most valuable employees work at your company?
- What are their career goals?
- What is their #1 career concern?
- How valuable are their skills in the market?
- Are they feeling fatigued and over-worked?
- Do they feel fairly compensated?
- Are they satisfied with their work — their colleagues — their projects?
- What do they like/dislike about their current assignment?
- What do they like/dislike about the organization's culture?
- What do they like/dislike about your management style?
- What are their personal interests — hobbies — family issues?
- What rewards mean the most to them?

Diversity

Diversity has to be treated as a positive. Because it *is* a positive. Diversity, it's true, does bring a greater demand for managerial sensitivity. But it also brings new ideas, fresh perspectives, new energy sources and new blood.

Lura Powell, formerly Director of a National Laboratory and the first woman to reach such a position in her field, feels strongly about this issue: "People often confuse diversity with EEO (Equal Employment Opportunity). But it's not enough, when you are leading an organization, to have a correct 'head count' of females and minorities. You need to let people operate in your organization as themselves. What happens all too often is an organization will hire people from different backgrounds and then try to change them — rather than realizing that because those people are different, they bring new strengths to the organization."

Or as another manager told me: "Sensitivity training is all well and good, but it's just the first step. You've got to focus on how to turn diversity into a positive, competitive advantage." Here are a few ways to do that:

- Link diversity with customer service. One obvious advantage of a diverse workforce is its ability to understand and be more responsive to the needs of a diverse customer base.
- Capitalize on diversity in problem-solving. People of all ages and from different backgrounds bring to the empowered workplace fresh ideas, opinions, perspectives and boundless creativity. It is the richness of the diverse perspectives, used in solving real business problems, that gives a company the innovative edge.
- Make diversity an explicit value of the organization — and hold people accountable for honoring that value. Then put values into action — when the company offers diversity training, make sure that senior managers are the first to attend and to discuss their personal challenges.
- Position diversity not as a "feel good" issue, but a business issue — the need to retain all talented employees.
- Sponsor organizational "associations" for various employee groups as an informal forum to express concerns, gain support, and share experiences.
- Promote unity. Ultimately, the talents, abilities, and perspectives of a diverse employee population must be united toward a common organizational objective, which challenges and rewards all who participate.

Training and Development

The workforce of the future is going to be increasingly computer literate. But that is probably the only positive thing that can be said about its educational attainment. America's public school system is in a woeful state today. According to the American Management Association, more than a third of job applicants tested in reading and math in 2000 lacked the basic skills necessary to perform the jobs they sought. Despite Generation X's high college graduate rate, American schools are turning out by the hundreds of thousands future employees who can neither read well enough to understand a personnel manager's questionnaire nor write well enough to fill it in intelligibly. Surveys have shown that more and more young people are joining the workforce each year without even a basic grounding in history, politics, arithmetic and English grammar. It isn't a matter of declining intelligence. It's a matter of declining educational standards — and that goes for college as well as high school graduates.

But blame isn't the issue for business leaders. The issue is how best to train and motivate a growing workforce that knows more about pop videos, computer games and TV soap operas than it does about self-discipline and basic learning skills. One thing for sure: workforce education pays off. Motorola estimates that it reaps $30 in profits for each dollar it spends on training.

Family Structures

Your family may have been nuclear, stable, well-housed, and financially secure. But that's *your* family. Statistics show that less than half of the families in America today can claim to match that profile. Which means that more than half of the men and women who make up today's workforce are dealing on a daily basis with problems and life situations that you may never have experienced.

According to figures published in 1960, 54 percent of American workforce families were "traditional" in structure — a breadwinner father, a homemaker mother and their 2.4 children under 18 years old. Dual breadwinner families in 1960 accounted for only 26 percent of the total workforce, single-parent breadwinner mothers numbered under 4 percent, single-parent breadwinner fathers counted for a scant 2 percent. By 1990, dual-breadwinner families had risen in number to 44 percent of the total workforce. Single-parent breadwinner mothers had trebled to nearly 12 percent. Single-parent breadwinner fathers had risen slightly to 3 percent, and the traditional breadwinner-father/homemaker-mother family had plummeted from more than half of the total workforce in 1960 to less than one-in-five (18 percent) in 1990. Today, two-income couples are becoming the norm. In 75% of U.S. households, both partners will work full time by 2005.

It is the practical problems arising from family restructuring that companies have to address most urgently. Personal services needs — housecleaning, child and elder care, janitorial work, gardening, home maintenance and repair, transport, even dog-walking — are increasing as dual-career families find less and less time to deal with domestic demands. Flexibility in work arrangements is increasingly crucial to retaining good employees. And this means accommodating less rigid work schedules for parents, allowing time off for child- and elder-care responsibilities, making space in the organization for job-sharing, permanent part-time employment, working from home options, and providing in-house counseling for problems ranging from mortgages to maternity issues.

Decision-Making

In a post-Enron era, the workforce is pretty skeptical about authority, and that skepticism is reflected in current attitudes toward corporate decision-making and goal-setting. Teamwork and other structural innovations in the 1980s and '90s went some way to bring middle and lower echelon workers into the decision-making process. But employees today demand an even greater say in how their companies set and execute goals, organize the workforce and distribute rewards. The workplace is becoming more volatile, as trust in authority declines and employees at all levels find the voice to express their own views. Technically savvy workers aren't waiting for the organizational chain of command to inform them of what's happening in the company. They are e-mailing each other, meeting in online chat rooms, and spreading information (and rumor) for all the world to see on cyber gripe and rogue web sites. Managers may find managing more difficult as a result, but the best are discovering means to turn those difficulties to their companies' and their workers' advantage by promoting greater commitment through greater participation.

The Ethics of Business

Allied to the workforce's deepening mistrust of authority is a growing spirit of concern for the effect of exploitative business behaviors upon individual, community and global well-being. Ethical issues, ranging from deceptive accounting practices to resource pollution, are already making newspaper headlines around the world. The day when workers, concerned only with job security, were prepared to see their companies make an extra buck from the destruction of a lake, an endangered species' habitat, or their own souls has long since passed.

Employees today — and certainly in the future — will only give their best to companies whose ethical visions they approve of and whose management practices encourage positive, responsible contributions that lead to more than just monetary reward. Workers want more than just a paycheck. They want their work to mean something; they want to feel valuable in themselves for what they do; and they want to feel that what they do adds value, however minutely, to the quality of their own, their colleagues' and the world's life.

This may sound like new age mumbo-jumbo. But believe me, it isn't. Ask the blue-collar worker who used to fish his local river weekends and can't now because the company he works for killed the river dumping toxic waste. Ask the working mother who's had to go on extended sick-leave because of work-related stress syndrome. Ask the employee who's had to seek counseling because of management bullying, or the senior vice president who discovered what peace of mind really means in a Buddhist ashram. Ask anybody you like. Concern for the environment, concern for society, concern for the individual, concern for spiritual and emotional well-being, concern for quality over quantity are all back on the American agenda.

Some of the world's largest corporations are taking the lead in responding to this agenda. Take DuPont, for example — a company in the process of transforming itself from an oil-and-chemicals giant into an eco-friendly life-sciences giant. It's goal is to own a collection of businesses that can go on forever without depleting natural resources. And DuPont is not alone in its concern for a range of socially responsible issues: UPS includes in its fleet some 1,800 alternative-fuel vehicles; Federal Express has a plan to convert all its trucks to hybrid electric-diesel engines; and Starbucks is buying more organic and shade-grown coffee, which minimizes disruption of rain forests. The Timberland Company allows workers to take a full week off each year, with pay, to help local charities. It also offers four paid sabbaticals (for up to six months) each year to employees who work full-time at a nonprofit. Just last year, 10 major banks, including Citigroup and Barclays, agreed to meet environmental- and social-impact standards when financing public works projects, such as dams and power plants, particularly in developing nations.

MEASURING EMPLOYEE MORALE

It may be difficult to gauge the exact amount of optimism/skepticism, affiliation/alienation, and trust/mistrust that permeate your workforce, but you *can* measure employee morale and job satisfaction — and when you find problem areas, you can openly address them. Here are a few questions you can start with:

1. On a five-point scale, where "1" is extremely dissatisfied and "5" is extremely satisfied, how satisfied are you with your present job?
2. On a five-point scale, where "1" is extremely dissatisfied and "5" is extremely satisfied, how satisfied are you with this organization?
3. On a five-point scale, where "1" is extremely low and "5" is extremely high, how would you rate the general level of employee morale?
4. Do you know what is expected of you on the job?
5. Do you know the long-term goals of the organization?
6. Does your supervisor respect you as a person?
7. Do you trust senior management to tell you the truth?
8. At work, are your opinions solicited, listened to, and sometimes acted upon?
9. On a five-point scale, where "1" is extremely likely and "5" is extremely unlikely, how likely do you think it is that you will be laid off within the next five years?
10. On a five-point scale, where "1" is totally out of touch and "5" is extremely in touch, how do you rate senior management's understanding of what employees think and feel about working here?
11. From your most objective viewpoint, are you compensated fairly for your work?
12. Do you believe that the senior managers of your company behave ethically?
13. Would you recommend this company to your friends if they were seeking employment?
14. Are you actively seeking employment outside this company?

Springfield Remanufacturing Corporation is an organization that prides itself on its participative work practices and high employee morale. When SRC distributed a questionnaire to be answered anonymously by its workforce, the responses "floored many of our managers," according to Jack Stack, the CEO. "The truth is, these types of morale problems are easy to miss, especially if you think you're doing well."

THE GHOST IN THE MACHINE

The term in Arthur Koestler's "Machine" refers to the human brain. "Ghost" names a hypothetical flaw in the brain's evolution that produced a split between reason and emotion as man advanced into the modern age. A similar split exists in too many American businesses today; a temperamental division between corporate goals and workforce needs that must be bridged if those businesses are going to remain front-line competitors in the new global economy. Changing workforce expectations arising from a radical realignment of American social values stand on one side of the divide. Corporate aims, driven by the need for greater efficiency and higher productivity, stand on the other. Neither side is going to win if each simply holds its ground, glaring across the chasm at its opponent, insisting upon the rightness and necessity of its own position. A compromise needs to be reached; a new model is required to replace the old Industrial Age vision of us-versus-them employer/employee relations. The ghost in the business machine is called intransigence. And the first step in exorcising intransigence will have been taken when worker and manager alike realize that a business actually isn't a machine at all, but a mutually dependent community of human beings.

2

THE NEW BUSINESS MODEL

"I thought we'd already found the right answer."

"We are in one of those great historical periods that occur every 200 to 300 years when people don't understand the world anymore, when the past is not sufficient to explain the future."

Peter Drucker

"**THE VOLATILE CONDITIONS** you're experiencing today aren't a temporary aberration," I tell my audiences. "They're real, they're fundamental and they're here to stay. You will never again shape a company or manage a workforce as you did in the good old days of corporate stability and predictable employee reactions. However brilliantly you may improvise, solutions to the challenges confronting you today cannot be constructed on the business models you grew up with. Those models no longer reflect reality. Stability is a thing of the past. And the time between surprises is shortening."

In the 16th century, the Polish astronomer Nicolaus Copernicus discovered that the earth revolves around the sun. With this simple observation, Copernicus created a heresy and a "revolution." The dethronement of the earth from the center of the universe called for the rethinking of almost every religious and scientific "truth" mankind had relied upon for the past 5,000 years. This wasn't just a paradigm shift, it was a paradigm shift on a grand scale.

Paradigms are simply agreed-upon models of the way things appear to work. But, as the Copernican revolution demonstrates, they are not immutable and they are not eternal. Paradigm shifts, as Thomas Kuhn explained in *The Structure of Scientific Revolution,* occur whenever the way we've been understanding the world is so in conflict with our experience of the world that the old model stops serving any useful purpose. It's when action based on a given model no longer produces the desired or expected results. The business world is experiencing such a shift today. Not because some Harvard economics professor proclaimed a fundamental error in our concept of business dynamics, but because business dynamics themselves have evolved beyond the model that gave rise to them 200 years ago. The forces that were discussed in the first chapter — the shift to a global economy, the impact of new technologies, the power of the consumer, the transition from the Industrial Age into the Knowledge Era, and the changes in the character of the workforce — have combined to dethrone past truths about organization, leadership, and business strategy. To paraphrase Peter Drucker, "The certainties of the past are no longer sufficient to inform the policies of the future."

The model on which all businesses have structured themselves since the Industrial Revolution derives from the laws of Newtonian physics. Its defining characteristic is its resemblance to a machine, and its longevity can be explained by the simple fact that up to about 30 years ago it worked. Then with the waning of the Industrial Age and the advent of the new global economy it stopped working. Predictions started going awry. Results began falling short of expectations. All kinds of practical problems began surfacing that could not be resolved by referral back to the old mechanical model.

At about the same time, corresponding anomalies were starting to surface in physics. The predictability of Newtonian science no longer dovetailed with new discoveries. The universe was not so orderly after all; chaos, it soon became evident, was an integral part of its makeup. "For the first time in 300 years," Fritjof Capra wrote in *The Turning Point*, "physicists faced a serious challenge to their ability to understand the universe. ... The new physics necessitated profound changes in concepts of space, time, matter, object, and cause and effect; and because these concepts are so fundamental to our way of experiencing the world, their transformation came as a great shock."

Today's business leaders are experiencing a similar shock with the breakdown of the old business model. But while the universe will go on running however physicists react to its newly discovered dynamics, businesses will not. "Many scientists," Thomas Kuhn wrote, "remain emotionally attached to theories that have long since been disproved. Ignoring overwhelming evidence, they will go to their graves stubbornly clinging to their limited but familiar points of view." Unfortunately, business leaders who follow that example are going to see their companies arrive at the graveyard long before they do.

THE NEW FOUNDATION

The problem I see most frequently today is the corporate struggle to revitalize workforces using a model of reality that no longer matches current workplace experience. If change *is* the new reality — and believe me, it is — then the only business paradigm that's going to produce positive results today is one that includes *insta-bility* as a positive element. Newton's rational, predictable universe is no longer our universe. Not in science or in business.

The foundation for both is shifting:

- From predictability to uncertainty;
- From linear progression to discontinuous leaps;
- From objective to subjective;
- From control to boundaries.

From Predictability to Uncertainty

In the Newtonian paradigm, all of nature was knowable through observation and the application of mathematical laws. This same view of reality formed the foundation for management practice in the Industrial Age. We operated with the conviction that there was always a right answer to be found. Our educational system rewarded those who found the one correct answer to questions. In business, if we couldn't find perfect solutions when we managed enterprises, we hired consultants who told us that they could. The organization was orderly and stable; disorder, variation and instability were viewed as counterproductive. Management's role in the linear, mechanical business model was to create predictability, stability, and control.

The arrival of quantum mechanics changed all that for Newtonian science, and similar circumstances are impinging on the business world today. New technologies, shifting customer preferences, unexpected government decrees come seemingly from nowhere, like unpredictable sub-atomic particles, to change some industries and make others obsolete. Change is no longer a force in the environment, it *is* the environment.

I don't mean to minimize the difficulty people have accepting the fact that uncertainty is normal and to be expected. But I do want to emphasize the fact that, difficult or not, uncertainty is the only dependable thing going for you today. A chief executive told me that managing in today's world was like working with wet clay: "The good part is that when clay is wet it is at its most pliable stage, which makes it a great time to mold totally new structures and ways of dealing with each other. The difficult part is that the clay never gets to dry — never gets to feel permanent — and this is very hard on people still drawn to the *illusion* of permanence."

And because (like it or not) the world *is* uncertain and unpredictable, companies need to share that complex and ambiguous reality with their employees. Leaders who continue to position their current strategy as the "right answer" to future challenges are encouraging employees to anticipate a spurious return to stability as soon as the correct structure/product-mix/staffing, etc. is in place. And when this state of permanence doesn't result — when the *next* "right answer" is announced and last year's strategy discarded — employees become more skeptical, more resistant, less trustful and less willing to believe that the company leadership has *any* idea of what is going on at all.

From Linear Progression to Discontinuous Leaps

Linear relationships are easy to think about. Nonlinear relationships are harder to grasp because they lack apparent logic. Discontinuity (nonlinear leaps in a transformation process) is intrinsically threatening. People can accept a certain amount of linear, incremental change because it makes sense to them, but discontinuous change provokes confusion and anxiety.

Benoit Mandelbrot's work with discontinuous equations in the 1960s showed the advantage of embracing discontinuity instead of struggling to resist it. He used nonlinear equations (repetitive loops that feed the answer back into the equation thousands upon thousands of times) to graph "fractal" designs. Besides being a more accurate representation of the world than the smoothed out cones and cylinders of traditional geometry, fractals lead to a positive appreciation of discontinuity as a source of reassurance that what first appears to be senseless irregularity, actually has an underlying order to it. By focusing on discontinuity rather than trying to smooth it out, fractals are now used to help understand formerly incomprehensible complex, chaotic systems like weather, the stock market, and even the level of violence or passivity in a population.

The same approach holds true for business today. We are experiencing discontinuity of epic proportions. Yet, when properly understood, discontinuity holds tremendous potential for creativity and growth. Charles Handy talks about discontinuity as an opportunity for learning: "Ask people to recall two or three of the most important learning experiences in their lives, and they will never tell you of courses taken or degrees obtained, but of brushes with death, of crises encountered, of new and unexpected challenges or confrontations. They will tell you, in other words, of times when continuity ran out on them, when they had no past experience to fall back on, no rules or handbook."

From Objective to Subjective

Under the old Newtonian paradigm, the nature of material reality was determined by what could be observed and measured. Objectivity became synonymous with Truth, and what could not be proven objectively was thought of as somehow hiding its "reality" from empirical scrutiny. A reasonable enough attitude when applied to subjects like astronomy or mechanics, but as British astrophysicist John D. Barrow pointed out in his *Theories of Everything*, "We had come to think of linear, predictable, and simple phenomena as being prevalent in Nature because we were biased toward picking them out for study."

Objective observation as the source of all knowledge was first questioned in the 19th century through the study of human psychology, and then given a real blasting in the 20th when quantum physicists studying the behavior of sub-atomic particles began to realize that the very act of observing interferes with that which is being observed. The physical inconsistencies that emerged when the same elementary matter was studied as particles in one experiment and as waves in another are a little difficult to grasp. But there is a story from zoology that makes the point clearly enough: A team of scientists photographing the mating habits of arctic seals at the North Pole discovered to their surprise that instead of simply getting on with it, the seals first dashed about the ice floes, clapping their flippers and bellowing hysterically until they were so exhausted they literally collapsed in each other's arms. Believing they had discovered something amazing about the sex lives of seals, the scientists showed their footage to a famous professor of zoology who, after a moment's thought, said simply: "And what would *you* do if you were in bed with your wife one night and a gang of strange-looking creatures walked in carrying movie cameras and spot lights?"

In our business organizations, we are only just beginning to comprehend what it means to move from a purely objective perspective to one that includes the intangible, subjective aspects of business. For example, "quality" was conceived as an objective, statistical concept — allowing only so many flaws per 1,000 or 1,000,000, and so on. Today, that thinking is being challenged by people like Charles Hampton Turner, a professor at the London Business School, who says: "There is no escaping the fact that a product or service can be no better, no more sensitive, esthetic or intelligent than are the relationships and communication of those who create the product or provide the service." If we follow Dr. Turner's statement to its obvious conclusion, quality moves from a purely statistical concept to a relationship issue. Rather than watching the numbers, companies should be looking at the basis of the relationships between customers and employees and between employers and employees. If those relationships are based in integrity and respect, then quality will naturally follow. The effectiveness and efficiency of an organization — its innovation, productivity, and quality — depend first on the strength of the relationships of its people.

Relationships are also viewed as an important part of employee satisfaction. Sue Swenson, the President of Leap Wireless International, says: "You can't lose sight of the fact that people thrive on social interaction. Employees are, first of all, social beings." Horst Schulze, former president and chief operating officer of Ritz-Carlton Hotels, agrees: "Employees come to work for two reasons: First to do a good job and to contribute to the organization, and secondly, to be with their co-workers, their friends. And by the way — these are the same reasons that I come to work."

Because the world of science was thought to be a material world, it ignored the existence of consciousness — of subjective experience, of values. When we extended the concept of duality to our organizations and management, we focused on quantifiable data and observable behavior and excluded or discounted the "non-measurable" dimensions of consciousness, emotion, and creativity. The separation of mind from matter has cost organizations their ability to engage and profit from the most potent, if invisible, gifts their employees have to offer. Only recently are organizations beginning to understand that the intangibles — employees' attitude, intuition, ideas, creativity, energy, and emotional engagement — are exactly what they need most to succeed in the future. Adds Horst Schulze, "When I speak with people in the different departments throughout the hotel, employees in every function, from dishwashing to marketing, have the same desire for the future — to be the best! This is the positive emotion and the kind of enthusiasm with which everyone starts out when a new hotel opens. The most important job of a leader is to keep that emotion and enthusiasm alive."

From Control to Boundaries

Chaos theory studies the relationship between order and disorder — states that are now viewed as being integral parts of a single whole — so that systems can react with apparent randomness and yet be held in bounds by forces that give them order. A system is defined as chaotic when there is no predictability to its next immediate action. But if the chaotic system is observed over a long enough period of time, a pattern arises in which certain boundaries are found to exist. The force that determines the shape of the system is called a "strange attractor," and although a system will never behave in exactly the same way twice, it will also never go beyond the pattern set by the strange attractor.

What creates boundaries in a *boundariless organization?* What facilitates decision-making when rules and regulations are reduced or eliminated? How do you control an organization in tumultuous times?

The answers to these questions call for radical re-definitions, not only of organizations, but the nature of control. Freedom becomes more important than control. Not freedom that is unlimited or irresponsible, but freedom within boundaries. By setting larger boundaries for employees, leaders find less for them to control. Leaders who influence us the most in the future will be those who understand that control is not about rules, regulations, and rewards — or the struggle to keep people "in line." When you think of the qualities that leaders need to encourage in their employees — responsibility, creativity, caring, commitment — you can see why coercion or manipulation just doesn't work.

The principle of the strange attractor shows that even the most erratic and complex system activity has an underlying order. Just as the magnetic influence of the attractor draws a chaotic system into a discernible pattern, so do strongly held values influence the judgements and actions of a workforce by creating a boundary beyond which behavior will not go. The most influential leaders are those who understand that guiding principles and organizational values play the central role in shaping workforce behavior today, not some list of rules and regulations.

I always take the following example of workforce empowerment with me whenever I address leadership conferences. It is the one-page *Employee Handbook* that Nordstrom, the Seattle-based retailer, gives its employees. By now, most business leaders are familiar with the handbook, but few of them have viewed the corporate value it embodies as an example of a strange attractor in action:

"Welcome to Nordstrom. We're glad to have you with our company. Our number one goal is to provide outstanding customer service. Set both your personal and professional goals high. We have great confidence in your ability to achieve them. Nordstrom rules: Rule #1 — Use your good judgement in all situations. There will be no additional rules. Please feel free to ask your department manager, store manager or division general manager any question at any time."

Can you think of a more potent prescription for chaos than inviting everyone in an organization to rely solely on good judgement — particularly their own interpretation of just what good judgement is — when making decisions? Yet Nordstrom's workforce does not disintegrate into thousands of employees "doing their own thing." Nordstrom's secret lies in stressing its primary corporate value — outstanding customer service — and then liberating employees' sense of responsibility *in service to* that value.

BUSINESS ORGANIZATIONS AS LIVING SYSTEMS

> "There is no such thing as merely surviving
> or maintaining the status quo in business. As in the
> organic world, there is only growth and decay,
> and growth is the business of business."
>
> **Isay Stemp, Editor,**
> *Corporate Growth Strategies*

Business leaders often speak to me about the need to create more intelligent, thoughtful, flexible, innovative, positively motivated organizations — organizations that can learn and adapt and relate constructively to changing situations and demands. I always tell them the same thing — that none of those characteristics can be found in a machine. They can only be found in *living systems.* Modeling a modern business structure on a clock or a car engine doesn't work anymore. What works today are organizational models derived from a living system. A jazz band, or a baseball team, or a coral reef. Even a flock of birds.

At a leadership conference for the International Association of Business Communicators, a living system metaphor was used to compare teamwork in the regional chapters with the behavior of a flock of geese:

- When geese fly in formation, they travel faster than when they fly at random.
- Geese share leadership. When the lead goose tires he (or she) rotates back down the "V," and another flies forward to become the leader.
- Geese keep company with the fallen. When a sick or weak goose drops out of flight formation, at least one other goose joins to help and protect.
- Being part of a team, we accomplish more, faster. Support, compassion and caring (honking from behind is the goose way) inspire those on the front lines, helping them to keep

pace in spite of pressure and fatigue. It is simultaneously a reward, a challenge, and a privilege to be a contributing member of a team.

The Living System Model of Transformation

Dissipative change is the process by which existing forms of any organization break up and seek entirely new forms and structures. The living systems model of transformation brings new perspectives for business organizations:

- Businesses are energized by fluctuations that in turn drive the processes of change.
- Organizations flourish at the edge of chaos — unstable, but not out of control.
- The free flow of information through the organization drives continuous improvement and innovation. Periodically, it also challenges and disrupts existing structures to create new forms of service delivery, levels of productivity and quality.
- Stability has a shorter life span, as processes temporarily manifest themselves in structures while they get ready for the next transformation. Managers facilitate the disorder.
- Constant experimentation becomes the norm. From a corporate mindset of "multiple right answers," local solutions are kept at the local level, and not elevated to models for the entire organization.
- A strong sense of identity and purpose keeps the workforce focused on a collective goal.
- People understand that progress is never a straight line. Uncertainties create the unexpected.
- The process of change is never over. Instead, change is valued as the creative dynamism, the very life of the system.

This is the model that makes sense of employees' actual experience and encompasses a rationale that will remain valid for the future. But I've discovered that the living systems model does even more than that. At the end of a recent program I delivered to an audience of scientists and engineers, I asked for questions and comments. One physicist raised his hand and said, "I like that change model a lot."

"Oh, you do?" I answered, assuming he liked it because he was familiar with the theories underlying it. Of course my assumption was wrong.

"Yes," he said cheerfully. "I like it because it's comforting."

MANAGEMENT INSIGHTS FROM A LIVING-SYSTEMS MODEL

Behaviors of living systems parallel and explain the behavior of a variety of social and human systems — organizations, management decision making, social behavior.

Insights from living systems include:

- There is creative potential in instability.
- Organizations thrive at the "edge of chaos."
- Information is the nutrient of the system.
- Organizational stability comes through a sense of identity and collective focus.
- Unintended consequences are to be expected.
- A large-scale reaction can result from a very small change.
- Self-organization changes management's role and relationship with workers.

This section of the chapter examines how these insights are being put to use today in business organizations around the world.

The Value of Instability

> "The winners of tomorrow will deal proactively with
> chaos, will look at chaos per se as the source of market
> advantage, not as a problem to be got around."
> **Tom Peters, *Thriving on Chaos***

Organic systems are adaptive; they don't just passively respond to events, they actively seek ways to take advantage of them. When Lars Kolind, the CEO of Oticon, wanted better products and stronger profits in his hearing aid manufacturing company in Denmark, he used instability as a way to establish an urgency for change. Kolind dissolved the entire formal organizational structure, did away with job titles and descriptions, and formed an in-house interior decoration committee to redesign headquarters with lounge areas, coffee bars and more open and casual work-floor arrangements. He declared that everyone should have a "multi-job" — their area of specialization *and* whatever else interested them. He created and focused the organization on the corporate slogan, "think the unthinkable." Kolind's efforts at Oticon caused a lot of confusion for employees who weren't sure how to react. Managers were told to recreate their jobs, but were not given instructions how to do it. Employees were left alone to sort out which people were best suited for working in this new kind of flexible and dynamic environment. Innovation was encouraged through unstructured gatherings where employees discussed, argued and debated. Risky? You bet. But at Oricon the risk paid off. This flat, dynamic structure, a knowledge-based "spaghetti organization," was especially suited for the realization of ideas. Employees developed the new processes and products that soon raised corporate profits. Today, Oticon consistently improves its position worldwide through new, technologically advanced hearing aids and a strong distribution network.

THRIVING ON THE EDGE OF CHAOS

"Jazz — like business — implies a series of balancing acts.
It must always be disciplined — but never driven — by
formulas, agendas, sheet music. It must always be pushing
outward, forward, upward — and therefore, inevitably,
against complacency."
John Kao, *Jamming*

It is essentially meaningless to talk about a complex adaptive system being in equilibrium because a system by nature is always unfolding and always in transition. However, a living system *can* manifest turbulence and coherence at the same time. I've said that instability is a critical element in the survival and transformation of all living systems, and yet in business we all know that too much instability can weaken an organization. If existing structures and interactions are to respond to environmental demands, the system must strike a balance between the need for order and the imperative for change. Complex living systems have evolved the ability to bring order and chaos into a special kind of dynamic balance called the "edge of chaos." The edge of chaos for business organizations is present when there is a balance between the traditional and the new, between order and freedom, between the need to maintain standards and the urge to experiment, and between the value of expertise and the input from fresh perspectives.

Skaltek AB is a Swedish company that designs, manufactures, and sells heavy machinery used by the wire and cable industry. Their custom-built machines — state-of-the-art and computer controlled — are sold in 40 countries around the world. Skaltek is not a traditionally structured organization in any sense: there are no titles, no supervisors, no janitors, no receptionists, no phone operators, no private secretaries, no sales or marketing department, and no quality control department. Instead, there is a community of peers, who are called "Responsibles" and who serve on teams which form and disband as necessary to fill customer orders or perform company projects. Chaotic? It certainly could be. But what keeps the dynamic balance at Skaltek is a corporate culture that includes the importance of each individual developing a personal vision (a sense of purpose in life that is inclusive of, but goes beyond, doing their job) and an organizational culture of personal accountability. All Responsibles coordinate their schedules with team members, visit customers, clean up after themselves (the plant is virtually spotless), and after assembling and testing a module that goes into a machine, affix a personally initialed aluminum label on the assembly which reads, "I'm Responsible." Skaltek's products enjoy a worldwide reputation of high quality, state-of-the-art design, and reliability.

The Power of Information

> "What they have found is truly startling …
> when you are born, you have all the information
> in your antibody system that you will ever need in your
> whole life to recognize anything you may encounter,
> including things that don't exist!"
> **Gerald Edelman,**
> **Nobel Prize winning biologist**

Information lies at the heart of natural life, lodged in the DNA. Life uses that information to organize itself into material form. Information is also the fuel of complex adaptive systems. In business, information flowing in and out, up and down provides the impetus that pushes the organization to transform. Leaders must be the champions of information access and sharing. As one consultant put it, "My most important function is to feed back organizational data to the whole organization. The data are often quite simple, containing a large percentage of information already known to many. But when an organization is willing to give public voice to that information — to listen to different interpretations and to process them together — the information becomes amplified. It grows and feeds on itself, building in significance."

Rather than a hierarchy, information-rich networked organizations are built on complex, mutually rewarding, and trusting relationships. Central control is not only impractical; it is becoming impossible to sustain. Instead of mandates passing through chains of command, we find streams of data and information flowing in every direction, empowering people to make their own decisions and adjust their actions according to a shared common purpose.

To really unify an enterprise, information has to be welcomed everywhere in the organization. The optimal culture is based on transparent communication that discloses its inner workings to everyone — not just to the upper echelon. In command and control cultures, people guard knowledge as their claim to power. Today's empowered workers need more information about the business. You cannot ask people to exercise broader judgement if their access to pertinent information is restricted.

When Oystein Skalleberg founded Skaltek, he intended to involve employees in all aspects of the business. Every Monday there is a company-wide meeting called "Information Cash Flow," at which workers get a full report of the previous week's sales, expenses, and profits. At Skaltek there are no financial secrets. If you interview employees at Skaltek, you'll hear people say, "I find it quite natural to know it all. If you work in the dark, you really don't know what you contribute."

Advances in information technology allow organizations to store and share key information quickly. Levi Strauss & Co.'s director of Employee Communications gave me her perception: "The first issue we identified when considering the value of an intranet — the ability to capture and share knowledge — was logical enough, but required some justification. Why *would* Levi place such a premium on capturing knowledge and creating a consistent platform of the best thinking across the company — and make a large investment in technology to do so? Because, while the process of making clothing is easy to grasp and the basic patterns haven't changed much in a long time, the marketplace *has* changed dramatically. In fact, it's constantly changing, always keeping us on our toes. Accordingly, the way we do business must keep pace with the changes happening all around us. Today, LS&CO. is a global enterprise operating in more than 60 countries. Competition is fierce everywhere we do business. Our success depends largely on continuous innovation and superior customer service. Both are fueled by a steady stream of knowledge throughout the company."

Stabilizing Through Identity and Collective Focus

> "One of the fundamental characteristics common
> to all living beings without exception is that of
> being objects endowed with a purpose."
>
> **Jacques Monod,**
> **Nobel Laureate and biologist**

In an open organization, where instability is embraced as positive, stability is maintained through corporate identity and collective focus of purpose. The leader's role is to create this stability through a constant reinterpretation of the company's history, present activities, and future aspirations. By doing this, leaders can allow all other activities to be mutable.

A corporate identity that reflects a constancy of purpose is a stabilizing force. Identity permeates the successful organization and is passed on to generations of workers through corporate legend and lore.

Nordstrom is one organization that does a remarkable job of using anecdotes about its sales force to communicate a value of impeccable customer service that is central to its identity. There is, for example, the often-repeated tale about the saleswoman who took her lunch hour to drive from downtown Seattle to the airport to make sure that her customer received his new business suit. The customer had purchased the suit that morning to wear at a meeting in another city the next day — and then discovered the garment needed alterations. The Nordstrom saleswoman, on her own initiative, had promised to have the suit altered and delivered to him before he left town. She kept her promise.

This story — and there are a lot more like it — is told to Nordstrom employees as an example of workforce "heroism." The success of this story-telling approach is evident with both internal and external audiences. To employees it demonstrates that they can go to almost any length to serve the customer and, not only will they be operating in good Nordstrom tradition, their stories may be used as heroic examples for others. To the public, these stories have created an awareness of Nordstrom's service mentality; even those who *don't* work there know the corporation's guiding values, and with rare exceptions, admire them enormously.

Unintended Consequences

> "I'm not afraid of death. It's just that I don't
> want to be there when it happens."
> **Woody Allen**

In the natural world, examples of complex adaptive systems include brains, immune systems, ecologies and ant colonies. In the social world they include political parties and business corporations. In each of these systems there is a network of individual "agents" acting in concert. In a brain the agents are nerve cells, enzymes, etc.; in a corporation the agents are departments, functions, individuals. Each agent functions in an environment produced by its interactions with other agents in the system. The relationships among agents are the conduits for the intelligence of the system. The more access people have to one another, the more possibilities arise for creating innovative solutions to challenges faced by the whole system. But within this myriad of actions, interactions, and shifting relationships, there also exist uncertainties and unintended consequences.

I was speaking recently to employees of a utility company in southern California and, because they wanted the entire workforce to attend, I spoke once in the morning and repeated the program in the afternoon. At the first session I had just finished covering the material on uncertainty and unexpected consequences when an audience member asked, "If everything is uncertain, what happens to strategic planning? How can you make any plans for the future?"

It was a good question, and I answered it by using the two sessions as an example:

"I was hired to put on two identical programs today, but you and I both know that it is impossible for them to be identical even though I will use the same set of PowerPoint slides for both presentations. The differences will be determined by the makeup of the two audiences — how many attend, what their energy level is, what questions they ask, maybe even what they had for lunch. And, of course, I too will be slightly different depending on my energy level and what I had for lunch, etc. I don't know *how* the afternoon session will be different, but I'm certain that the unexpected will happen."

What all this means to me as I prepare for programs — and what this means to a company as it prepares for the future through strategic planning — is that we have to make our plans taking into account a multitude of contingencies in a volatile environment. And then we've got to understand that, despite our best efforts, the future may or may not play out the way we anticipated. We need to keep reorienting as conditions change frequently in unexpected ways. The trick is not to let the unexpected throw you. It's just part of the game.

The Butterfly Effect

*"Change takes infinitesimal differences ...
and blows them up in your face."*
James Crutchfield, physicist

In 1960, meteorologist Edward Lorenz created a computer model that simulated weather patterns. In his book, *Chaos,* James Gleick talks about the inception of this model: "With his primitive computer, Lorenz had boiled weather down to the barest skeleton. Yet, line by line, the winds and temperatures in Lorenz's printouts seemed to behave in a recognizable earthly way. They matched his cherished intuition about weather, his sense that it repeated itself, displaying familiar patterns over time, pressure rising and falling, the air stream swinging north and south... But the repetitions were never quite exact. There was a pattern, with disturbances. An orderly disorder."

By the 1980s, supercomputers with advanced versions of computer modeling changed the weather business from an art to a science. Nevertheless, beyond two or three days, the world's best forecasts were still speculative, and beyond six or seven days, they remained essentially useless. The "Butterfly Effect" was the reason. Technically called *sensitive dependence on initial conditions,* the Butterfly Effect demonstrates how tiny discrepancies at the beginning of a system's evolution make accurate prediction of its outcome impossible. The Effect is so named because of the hypothesis that the way in which a butterfly flaps its wings in Brazil could eventually cause a hurricane on the East Coast of the United States.

In all dynamic systems, like weather, there are inescapable consequences emerging from the way very small events intertwine with large ones. "For want of a nail, the kingdom was lost," refers to a sequence of events beginning with a relatively minute one (the lost nail), which resulted in the horse throwing a shoe, which resulted in the rider being bucked off, which resulted in the battle being lost, and then eventually the entire kingdom. All because of a missing nail.

Such disproportionate relationships between cause and effect often defy management's best efforts to predict and control. What looks like a solution today may result in a larger problem tomorrow. You can prepare for potential "Butterfly challenges" by continually scanning your surroundings, retrieving data, and turning it into knowledge on which to base new decisions. You cannot possibly anticipate all of the potential leverage points in your organization, but you can stay alert for the first signals of overreaction (by continually getting feedback from customers, suppliers, employees, competitors) so that you can respond rapidly.

The Capacity for Self-Organization

> "The notion of self-organization in human systems may suggest to some that the manager has no real role. The reality is that management has a different role; rather than controller, the manager becomes a liberator."
>
> **L. Douglas Kiel,**
> ***Managing Chaos and Complexity in Government***

Complex systems are comprised of many independent agents interacting with each other in many ways. It is the very richness of these interactions that allows the system as a whole to undergo spontaneous self-organization: Atoms form chemical bonds and become molecules, birds adapt to the behaviors of their neighbors and organize themselves into flocks, teams transcend themselves to become more than the sum of their individual parts. In every case, it happens without a blueprint or conscious plan. The realm of computer networks is a created world, built on an intentionally organic, anarchy-inspiring skeleton. Groups form around their special interests, linking people from every conceivable background and demographic segment. Just as there is no master neuron in the brain, no single computer in the internet "web" means more than another. To create a business around a living system model is to give an organization the freedom to realize its organic capacity to self-organize without any externally imposed plan or direction. This means that leaders have to believe that the workforce has the innate ability to respond to continuous change, to create temporary structures and relationships as required, to experiment, and to find simplified and more effective ways to get results.

Xerox Corporation found the value of self-organization when it was looking for a way to boost the productivity of its field service staff. A cultural anthropologist from the Xerox Palo Alto Research Center (PARC) traveled with a group of tech reps to observe how they actually did their jobs — as opposed to how they described what they did, or what their managers assumed they did. The anthropologist discovered that the reps spent more time with each other than with customers. They'd gather in common areas like the local parts warehouse or around the coffee pot and swap stories from the field. An old model company manager would have viewed the time spent socializing as a "gap" to be eliminated for higher productivity, but the anthropologist saw the exact opposite.

For Xerox, the informal gatherings didn't represent time wasted, but rather money in the bank. For it was here, within these self-organized *communities of practice,* that the reps asked each other questions, identified problems, and shared new solutions as they devised them. And it was through conversations at the warehouse — conversations that weren't part of any formal "business process" or reflected in any official organizational chart — that knowledge transfer took place. Thanks to their anthropologists, Xerox is now experimenting with "elegantly minimal processes" that create more room for local interpretations and innovations, so that more effective business practices can evolve naturally from the grassroots upward, as they should, rather than being imposed from above.

Fritjof Capra writes: "Self-organizing systems … tend to establish their size according to internal principles of organization, independent of environmental influences. This does not mean that living systems are isolated from their environment; on the contrary, they interact with it continually, but this interaction does not determine their organization."

Self-managed teams, encouraged to keep their membership "fluid" — to form, adjust the size and composition of the group, even to decide when to disband — follow these same principles. A problem-solving exercise divided management staff into several teams and assigned each to prepare simulated bidding on a government bond auction. Some teams were set up with the same people working together throughout the experiment. In other teams, the membership was fluid; people left or were added as seen necessary by the group. The fluid group of teams produced a higher error rate initially, but over time made fewer mistaken decisions. The teams with rigid membership became inhibited by their more limited and structured view of the problem, with the result that fewer alternatives and solutions were produced. The "unstable" teams promoted more divergent outcomes and were more readily adaptive to changing situations.

Self-organization changes the role of leaders

It is inevitable that formal hierarchies become less important as people gain increased access to information and begin naturally to seek leadership from whoever has the necessary knowledge or experience. In a self-organized system where leaders emerge organically from situation to situation, it becomes necessary to develop leadership skills in employees throughout the organization. The National Collegiate Athletic Association has created a professional development program for NCAA staff. The Team Academy is based on the idea that true empowerment requires leadership to occur in every position within the organization, and that *everyone* in today's workforce must have prepared him or herself to accept the responsibilities and accountability for leading others.

As organizations subscribe to a living-system model, the criteria for leadership changes. Developing leaders for this self-organized workforce is very different from developing managers for a bureaucracy. Leaders today have to be teachers, facilitators, supporters, coaches, counselors, and storytellers.

In the business world today, as in nature, change can destroy organisms that aren't adaptive. And adaptive organizations must be staffed by adaptive individuals. In a world where flux is the norm, leaders need a workforce with the attitudes and skills that allow it to cope with the continuous flow of new ideas, products, markets, and perspectives. The next chapter looks at how to spot and develop change-adept employees.

3

THE CHANGE-ADEPT WORKFORCE

"I know I need to change, but I don't know if I can."

"People who deal effectively with change tend to have a well-developed self-image and a high degree of self-confidence in their skills and abilities. They know that the world is moving at a much faster pace than it did 10 or 20 years ago, when many of them started their business careers. They have come to accept change as a reality — a fact of business life. Some of them, the best of them, thrive on it. They like the challenge: it's stimulating and energizing. And those are the people who we ultimately need as leaders throughout this organization. If people can't accept change, they are going to have a difficult time. Not just here, and not just in this industry, but anywhere, and in so many aspects of life."

Ron Cooper, COO, Adelphia Communications

I HAVE A PSYCHOLOGY BACKGROUND, and in my private practice I counseled hundreds of people who were having problems adjusting to the effects of downsizing and organizational restructuring. (This kind of case became so common that I built a reputation by specializing in helping individuals deal with change.)

When I began giving speeches and seminars to organizations, much of my preparation centered on research into what distinguishes the kinds of people who deal successfully with change from those who can't, or won't. I've spoken on this topic to client organizations in 19 countries around the world during the past 20 years — and my research files are still growing.

Just as some organizations cannot survive in a continuously changing environment, some individuals find themselves emotionally overwhelmed when faced with the need to constantly refocus on new roles and situations. These "victims" of change often misdirect their energy by railing against things they cannot hope to influence while fixating on the negative aspects of an uncertain future. They lose heart and look for places to lay blame while abdicating personal responsibility. Longing for stability and certainty, they embody what I call a "Whitman Sampler" mentality. (The Whitman company prints a guide to the candy on the inside of its Sampler box cover.) If life is like a box of chocolates, then these are the people who want a map to the selection inside — and they want the map to be right!

At the opposite end of the spectrum are people whom I've labeled "change-adept." These individuals deal with change exceptionally well and are naturally happier in their work because they have come to terms with a world that never stays the same. They move with today's chaotic workplace, rather than fighting against it. They are energized by and actually thrive on change.

The change-adept are not necessarily more competent than their less-adventurous co-workers, but they have distinct advantages in the attitudes they hold and the strategies they adopt. Change-adept professionals build greater resilience and not only survive, but flourish in changing times. (At Kinsey Consulting Services, we have developed a "Change-Adept Questionnaire" that assesses an individual's current attitudes, aptitudes, and skills for thriving on change. You can find it on my web site: www.CKG.com.)

If leaders are going to take a workforce successfully into a future of unknowns, the value of having change-adept employees cannot be overstated. This chapter tells how to spot the change-adept professionals in your organization and how to create an environment that encourages change-adeptness in the entire workforce.

PROFILE OF CHANGE-ADEPT PROFESSIONALS

Basically, I have found six factors that determine which people deal successfully with change. The six factors are:

- Confidence
- Challenge
- Coping
- Counterbalance
- Creativity
- Collaboration

Factor #1 — Confidence

The personality trait most responsible for an individual's ability to deal well with change is self-confidence. Confident people are self-motivated, have high self-esteem, and are willing to speak up and to take risks. Quite simply, they know how good they are.

In the workplace, self-confident employees are often those who feel secure in the portability of their skills, whose professional networks are intact, and who know they will survive professionally, even if it means finding a new position or a new employer. They recognize their value to the organization and have a realistic perception of their worth in the marketplace. Because they focus on their strengths and strive to develop their talents, they have an obvious advantage over those who may be equally talented, but fixate on their limitations and are paralyzed by setbacks. But even the most confident of employees may suffer a crisis of self-doubt in times of change, and it is here that leadership awareness and assistance become critical strategy issues.

Leadership Strategy — Play to People's Strengths

Competence, strangely enough, bears little relationship to confidence. The fact that people on your staff do their jobs very well does not, by itself, insure that they are also confident of their abilities. It is only when people are *aware* of their competence that they become confident.

Lee Strasberg, the famous acting coach, said, "I can train you in anything except that for which you have no talent." Everyone has areas of lesser and greater talents, and while it can be helpful to acknowledge weaknesses and seek guidance or training to develop those areas, there is nothing more frustrating than to strive vainly to excel in areas of endeavor where one has little or no natural ability.

Talents overlooked may atrophy, and weaknesses — regardless of how much effort is put into trying to improve them — will never match a person's natural strengths. Management expert Peter Drucker advises, "Don't focus on building up your weaknesses. Understand your strengths and place yourself in positions where those strengths can best be employed. Your strengths will carry you through to success."

We know intuitively that Dr. Drucker's advice is sound, but leaders seldom follow it in the workplace. Instead, most workers report that they are singled out for notice only when there is a problem with their performance. Here is a question I often ask my audiences: "If your boss told you that she noticed something about your performance and wanted you to come to her office to discuss it, would you assume that she had noticed an area of your special competence and wanted to bring it to your attention?" Among the majority of audience members who respond with nervous laughter, only a few hands raise.

Bosses tend to notice and comment on weaknesses and mistakes more than they comment on talents and strengths. Bosses feel it is their role to criticize because the old model for employee improvement is based on what one middle manager refers to as the "If-I-don't-say-anything, you're-supposed-to-know-you're-doing-fine. I'll-let-you-know-if-you-screw-up." mentality. While continuous learning and self-improvement are valid concepts for future success, focusing solely on what is lacking leads to an unbalanced evaluation of employees' worth and potential. It is no wonder then that most workers have problems taking risks and confronting uncertain situations. The focus is on weakness, not competence, and without an awareness or confirmation of their strengths, workers lack the confidence required to embrace change.

Focusing on employees' strengths takes a management strategy that includes the following:

- **Don't assume people know how good they are.**

I gave a speech to the top management team of a software company in northern California that was relocating out of state. A few days later the president of the company telephoned me to say, "After your presentation last week, I began thinking. I have an administrative assistant who is probably the brightest, most creative person I've worked with. The problem is, she's married and can't move her family out of the Bay Area. I was wondering if you would see her for a private counseling session, so that when she applies for a new job, she will come across just as terrific as she really is. I'll even pay for the session."

Of course, I agreed, and looked forward to meeting this talented woman. When she came into my office I said, "This is a real pleasure. I've heard so many nice things about you. Tell me about yourself. What is it that you do exceptionally well? What would you most want a prospective employer to know about you?" The woman was silent for several seconds. Finally she sighed and said, "I really don't know. I do a lot of things well, but when I do them, I don't notice."

• **Notice when employees do something very well, and acknowledge it immediately.**

Timing is everything when it comes to building talent and strengths. Get in the habit of commenting on outstanding employee behavior as soon as you notice it. When managers at a California restaurant chain catch a worker doing something exceptional, they immediately give the employee a "Star Buck." Each restaurant has a monthly drawing from the pool of stars for prizes (cash, TVs, etc.), and each region has a drawing for $1,000 cash.

• **Encourage employees to recognize their own achievements and then to "go public."**

One manager I know came up with a creative solution to her employees' lament that, although she did a pretty good job overall, there were many times when she seemed too preoccupied to notice accomplishments. The manager put a hand-painted sign in her office and jokingly encouraged employees to display it whenever they had a significant achievement. What started out as an office gag is now a favorite employee ritual. The sign reads, "I just did something wonderful. Ask me about it!"

• **Help employees identify strengths and then find ways to capitalize on them.**

Sometimes a person's strengths aren't being utilized to the fullest. Everyone has unique talents and abilities that are not always used in their present jobs. When Paula Banks worked as Human Resources Director at Sears, she had a secretary who was doing an adequate, but mediocre job. Paula talked to the woman and found out that, in her spare time, she was a top salesperson for Mary Kay Cosmetics. In Paula's words: "I found out she had great sales skills, so I changed her duties to include more of what she was really good at — organizing, follow-through, and closing deals. She had this tremendous ability. My job was to figure out how to use it."

- **Set "stretch" goals that pull employees beyond previous levels of achievement.**

A former director of recruitment for the United States Coast Guard said that the branch of the service best known for building confidence in its members is the Marine Corps. In his opinion, the reason is that boot camp training constantly challenges Marine recruits to perform beyond their previous physical limits. As a result, there is tremendous pride in passing tests of rigorous standards and being found capable.

Most managers I spoke to agreed. They told me that the more they challenge their teams, the more people "pull up" for it. And when they do — when they actually accomplish the "impossible" — people begin to realize they are capable of achieving more than they'd ever thought.

- **Create small victories.**

To encourage people on the way to achieving goals of exceptional performance, managers need to design "small wins." One executive put it this way: "A stretch goal can scare people to death. I always begin with a mini-goal that I know my staff can achieve, and then I use that victory as a confidence-builder for reaching the larger objective."

- **Give *all* employees the opportunity to discover their abilities.**

The Office Support Network (OSN) is an inner-company organization of office and clerical workers at S.C. Johnson Wax. Reporting to the head of Human Resources, it has a 10-member steering committee and nine subcommittees that address the growth and development of office staff. When I addressed the OSN at their annual dinner meeting, the chairwoman of the steering committee (also a library clerk) hired me and made all the financial and travel arrangements for my engagement. Her experience with the OSN greatly enhanced her opinion of her abilities: "This program has given me a whole new view of myself. I now know that I can conduct meetings and give speeches. For the first time, I feel that I'm a true professional with a lot to offer."

- **Spend less time on what needs to be improved.**

Todd Mansfield, Executive Vice President of Disney Development Company, found that his company had been spending too much time on employee weaknesses: "When we'd sit down to evaluate associates, we'd spend 20 percent of our time talking about the things they did well, and 80 percent on what needed to be improved. That is just not effective. We ought to spend time and energy helping people determine what they are gifted at doing and get their responsibilities aligned with those capabilities."

- **Spend more time on developing potential.**

Play to individual strengths. At Reell Precision Manufacturing Corporation, performance reviews are designed solely to help employees find and develop their potential. The biggest change Reell made was to disconnect the review from any connection to pay. Now the entire focus of the session is on what employees are currently doing and how to help them develop their potential.

Leadership Strategy — Reward Failure

Some individuals and enterprises would rather run from uncertainty, but they cannot. In a chaotic world, many of the best routes to success require great risks. Companies attempt radical work reform which can boost productivity and cut costs but have a high failure rate: they pursue cutting edge technological innovations that may or may not take hold; they invest in deregulated industries that offer potentially good profits, but with the certainty of intense competition; and they expand into fast-growing developing countries that offer the most lucrative opportunities coupled with the greatest risks.

We need to appreciate that new knowledge comes as much from failure as it does from success. Understanding what doesn't work may be at least as important as understanding what does, provided these failures are revealed early in a project and are swiftly reexamined. Learning from failure is a boon at this point: Few resources have been committed and decision making is flexible, meaning that other approaches can themselves be tested.

Tom Watson, Sr., the founder of IBM, was often quoted as saying, "The way to accelerate your rate of success is to double your failure rate." A manager I know says, "I tell my folks to make at least 10 mistakes a day. If they're not making 10 mistakes a day, they're not trying hard enough."

When people make mistakes or fail in some attempt, self-doubt can become overwhelming. That's human nature. It isn't that change-adept professionals are never afraid or doubtful, it is just that they don't let their fears stop them from taking action. Part of their resilience is a philosophy that views failure in a unique way. The change-adept impressed me with their refusal to consider mistakes as defeats. A typical point of view was: "The word *failure* is not in my vocabulary. When I make a mistake, it is just a breakdown showing me exactly what needs to be looked at before I continue along the path — but I am always on the path."

"Failure is not a crime. Failure to *learn* from failure is," said Walter Wriston, the former chairman of CitiCorp. Leaders can begin to develop a workforce of confident risk-takers by encouraging and learning from failure. Some organizations actually reward mistakes with a quarterly failure trophy. The failed efforts must have been ethically sound, recognized as failures quickly, and learned from thoroughly.

Another way to encourage risk-taking in others is to use your own personal failures as constructive examples. Talk openly and honestly about your errors and setbacks — and what you learned as a result. Let people know that you took risks when you were afraid and unsure of the outcome. The general manager of an insurance company, concerned that her salespeople were so afraid of failure that they hesitated to take even well-calculated risks, took action at a sales meeting. She put two $100 bills on the table and related her most recent failure, along with the lesson she had learned from it, then she challenged anyone else at the meeting to relate a bigger failure and "win" the $200. When no one spoke up, she scooped up the money and said that she would repeat her offer at each monthly sales meeting. From the second month on, the manager never again got to keep the $200, and as people began to discuss their failures, the sales department became more successful, quadrupling their earnings in one year.

Leadership Strategy — Build an "Unlearning Organization"
Employees can become psychologically attached to the status quo because it is familiar and comfortable. But even more difficult than fighting off the inertia of comfort, people find it hard to let go of the past because it is there that they experienced personal success. Almost everyone likes the experience of mastery — of knowing they are doing a good job. That's understandable, that's basic human psychology — it's just not an attitude that helps companies move forward. Although it might have been a valid assump-

tion in the past, when companies valued employees for their entrenched knowledge, the reality of a high-speed future is that current knowledge quickly becomes outdated. Now employees are valued *less* for what they know and more for how quickly they can *learn*. In addition, one of the greatest challenges of a learning organization is to help employees identify those practices that they need to *unlearn* in order to more quickly adopt new behaviors. Leaders must help staff use past competencies, not as a reason to *stop* learning, but as a springboard to future success.

Business leaders who help employees to "unlearn" address the issue directly: They talk about their own problems with unlearning, they empathize with the feelings of awkwardness that people have when leaving their "comfort zone," and they massage damaged egos by applauding the efforts that are being made.

Building a style of corporate behavior that is comfortable with — even aggressive about — new ideas, risk, change, and failure, means that workers need to change their attitudes about incompetence. Unlearning — and doing it quickly — is the key to rapid advancement. Instead of labeling incompetence as something to avoid, it should be embraced for what it really is — a positive sign of unlearning. Here are a few questions about learning and unlearning that all employees should be asked to consider:

- What do I do best? (What skills and abilities am I most proud of?)
- Which current skills, abilities, and attitudes will continue to make me successful in the future?
- How does feeling competent stop me from doing things differently? (Where are the "comfort zones" that I'm most reluctant to leave?)
- What new skills do I need to learn to stay valuable to the organization?
- What have I learned in the past six months?

- What do I expect to learn in the next six months?
- What do I need to unlearn? (Which skills are becoming obsolete? What practices — attitudes, behaviors, work routines, etc. — that worked for me in the past are no longer valid?)

Leadership Strategy —
Build Employees' Work Security

Marketplace realities dictate that employees become their own career managers — assessing their strengths and weaknesses, developing personal goals, benchmarking proficiencies, tracking industry and market trends, planning for retirement, and building a portfolio of skills that is transferable to other work situations. As people build "career resilience," they develop an inner security that provides the resources to take care of themselves, even if the company doesn't, or can't.

In developing career resilience, employees need the assurance that they'll be told the criteria for success in the future — that the skills, attitudes, etc. they will need will be clearly communicated — and that assistance in preparing will be available. Leaders endeavoring to foster career resilience have come up with constructive programs in response:

- USS-POSCO, a joint venture with South Korea and U.S. Steel located in northern California, has a Learning Center offering free night school courses to all employees. Some of the courses are directly job-related; others, like stress-reduction and pre-retirement planning, help employees take control of their future.
- The Regional Municipality of Ottawa offers employees the opportunity to try out short-term assignments in areas of interest at levels higher than the ones they presently occupy, or perhaps even in totally different fields where

they can explore and apply transferable skills. The Development Assignment for Regional Employees (DARE) program allows employees to work for a period of up to six months in other parts of the organization at their same salaries and without fear of penalty if failure occurs.

Leadership Strategy —
Give Employees "Exit Power"

Several years ago, I spoke at a business convention in Dallas, Texas. I arrived early to see how the meeting room was set up and to observe the audience reaction as they listened to the speaker on the program ahead of me. I don't recall the speaker's name, but I remember his closing comments: "My topic this afternoon has been *power*, and I've spoken about several kinds of power, including 'positional power' which has to do with your title and level in the organization, and 'information power' which comes from your knowledge or access to information. However, there is one kind of power I haven't addressed, yet, and without it you will never enjoy any other kind of power in your organization. It is 'exit power.' If you haven't thought through and developed a plan of action for what you would do if you were fired — written an up-to-date draft of your resume, developed a solid network of business contacts, saved enough money to survive unemployment for several months — then you don't have exit power."

Leaders build workforce confidence and loyalty by helping employees develop exit power. I consulted for an oil company at the beginning of its reengineering effort, and during a meeting with the change task force, we began to discuss the drop in confidence the workforce was experiencing. One of the managers shook her head. "Not my staff," she said. "Everyone in my department is doing just fine." When we asked her why they were doing so well, the manager said that every week she brought her team together and spent an hour or more going over strategy for various organizational contingencies. "We look at the current changes going on in the business and the changes we anticipate in the future, and then we plan how best to position ourselves for all outcomes. We plan our personal financial and career strategies, we share information and leads about open positions throughout the company, we've even planned a response if our entire function is eliminated. We've decided to stay intact as a department and to sell our services back to the organization."

One leader I know took another novel approach to building employee confidence during a time of organizational upheaval. As a senior vice president of a national bank during a takeover bid by another bank, Norm's department was more productive, and his employee retention rate higher than that of other departments. Norm said to me, "I know how unnerving it is not to know what will happen in the future. I understand how confidence levels drop under these conditions. One thing that works for me personally is to give my resume to corporate headhunting firms. It's not that I'm looking to change companies, it's just that I need the confidence that comes only with knowing how desirable I am in the marketplace." He continued, "You know what else I've done? I've told all my managers to circulate their resumes as well."

Factor #2 — Challenge

In Chinese, the ideogram for *crisis* combines two characters: One is the symbol for danger, the other for opportunity. The same dual aspects can be ascribed to change. With any change, the danger of possible reversals coexists with incredible opportunities for personal and professional success. Leaders need employees to look for the opportunities in change.

When change-adept people are asked for verbal images they associate with change, they acknowledge the stress, uncertainty,

pressure, and disruption, but they also emphasize the benefits —
the opportunity, growth, adventure, excitement and challenge.

Long before Dale Carnegie, the human potential movement, or
self-help videos, a positive outlook was acknowledged to be a crucial part of high-level achievement. Cynicism is rampant in organizations, but it occupies little space in the outlook of change-adept
individuals. In a fast-moving, high-stress business environment, a
positive, upbeat, "can-do" attitude is vital for success.

While the change-adept do not dwell on negativity, they are
not oblivious to potential danger. Rather, they analyze situations for
both positive and negative aspects, develop strategies to minimize
negatives and optimize positives, and then focus on the upside of
the situation. Change-adept individuals realize that spending too
much time worrying about troublesome aspects or negative outcomes is a waste of mental energy that saps enthusiasm and makes
it more difficult to realize the potential opportunities that are also
inherent in the situation.

People in an organization who assimilate to change and seek
to become involved in it tend to have a much higher self-image
when that wave of change has passed. Those who are swept along,
either unwilling or unable to contribute to the change, are left feeling unsatisfied and disappointed in the way change controlled
them. Obviously, people cannot control all that happens to them at
work, but everyone can control how they *respond* to what happens.
When will the business stabilize? It won't. Change is with us and
will be with us for the rest of our working lives. No one can escape
that fact.

So where does that leave us? I think it leaves us in a similar situation to that in which Winston Churchill found himself when he
visited Canada. At a cocktail party, Churchill stood next to a bishop
of the church when a lovely young woman passed out glasses of

sherry. Churchill took a glass and then the woman offered a drink to the bishop, who refused by saying, "I would rather commit adultery than have a drop of liquor touch my lips." At which point Churchill replied, "Ask the young lady to return. I didn't know we had a choice."

Change-adept people know they have a choice. If change is indeed a fact of life, it is just a fact. And facts are external, objective events over which they may have little or no influence. But reaction, attitudes, and the positive or negative labels they give the facts — all of these are factors over which the change-adept exerts choice and control.

Leadership Strategy —
Accentuate the Positive

Change is difficult for the people going through it. Change challenges deeply held assumptions and beliefs about careers, personal talents, and the organization's future. It's no wonder that even talented, intelligent employees face change with some misgivings and negativity. A critical element in developing a change-adept workforce is understanding how to encourage optimism throughout the workforce.

Dr. Henry Goddard, when he was the psychologist at Vineland Training School in New Jersey, measured fatigue in children after criticism and after praise. When they were praised, there was an immediate upsurge of new energy that increased performance. When they were criticized, the children's energy plummeted.

Further studies on motivation with adults found that telling a group of people they did poorly on solving 10 puzzles decreased their performance on a second try. Telling the group it did well — regardless of whether the praise was deserved — improved performance on a second try.

I'm not suggesting that you praise people when they do nothing to deserve it, but it is instructive to note that criticism is rarely constructive, and praise is almost always energizing and motivating. If you want to develop optimistic employees, praise and thank them for a job well done. Let people know how much you honor and appreciate their contributions to the organization. Even if those contributions are negligible, nothing is gained — and much may be lost — by openly criticizing employees you plan to retain in your workforce. If criticism is called for, do it privately and with compassion.

Leadership Strategy —
Give Good People the Bad News

Because leaders perceive today's workforce to be more cynical and less optimistic than that of previous generations, they often make a big mistake in their communications. They tend to present factual information about the organization with a too-positive spin — commenting solely on the most positive aspects to wary employees. Not only is this misguided communication strategy out of step with the reality that employees experience, it further widens the trust gap between leaders and workers. ("Are these executives working in the same company that we are?")

Most importantly, a diet of all good news does not motivate employees to be more positive and upbeat. Instead of helping develop optimism, the lack of full disclosure actually encourages the rumor mill to fill in the missing communication, often by inventing or distorting information in ways that exacerbate workforce apprehension.

A much more effective communication strategy is to level with employees about the current problems and challenges the company is facing so they will have a complete picture of the situation. I was speaking at a meeting sponsored by the Conference Board, and sitting on the same panel of experts was the head of corporate communications from Weyerhauser Corporation. He said that the local newspaper had printed a negative story about the company and its environmental policies. After meeting with senior management, it was decided to rerun the news story in their in-house magazine, and next to the negative article to print the company's point of view. The result was that employees were treated as adults, not sheltered like children. They were given both sides of the story and trusted to draw their own conclusions.

Factor #3 — Coping

In an environment of constant flux, intellectual capital steadily depreciates. I address this issue in my programs when I tell audiences, "What you know about your industry is worth less right now than when I started this speech. Customer needs have changed, technological progress has raced ahead, and competitors have advanced their plans. Now and for the future, your value to the company increasingly depends less on what you currently know, and more on how quickly you can update your knowledge in response to changing conditions."

Some people are naturally more flexible and better at coping with and adapting to a complex, fast-paced reality than others. These individuals take charge of change by accepting responsibility and assuming control. A few years ago, at a management meeting in Canada for the Saskatchewan Government Insurance Company, an audience member approached me and said, "What I liked best about your speech was the part about the importance of personal flexibility to deal with change. That's because my father was the head of the Canadian prison system, and he developed a test that was the mark of the criminal mind. Would you like to hear about it?"

I said that I was very interested, so he continued, "It was really simple. My father would bring each prisoner into his office and sit across from him at a table that had two colored lights — a red one and a green one. My father operated the lights from switches that were hidden under the table. The prisoners' task was simple — when the red light flashed, they were to touch the red light, and when the green light went on, they were to touch the green. All the prisoners could do that just fine, but what none of them could do — so predictably that my father referred to the trait as 'the mark of the criminal mind' — was to see the red light flash and begin to move their hands in that direction, and then see the green light go on and alter course in time to touch the green light. "

The man waited for my reaction. "You see?" he said. "No flexibility. They couldn't commit to one action and then change course when appropriate. But of course, these were the criminals who'd been caught — the ones who couldn't deviate from set plans even when things weren't working out."

The lesson this story highlights is that the new business environment requires organizations to create the capacity for rapid decision-making. It's also critical that decisions are made in a way that keeps options open. A strong corporate culture can prove to be counter-productive if the emphasis is on stability. A culture that does not encompass organizational fluidity can "lock in" and inhibit change, making the system dangerously vulnerable. A critical element in the health of any organism is robustness: the ability of a system to absorb small jolts. To create a robust organization, you must build flexibility and resilience into its foundation.

In chaotic times, the trick is not to brace for change, but to loosen up and learn how to roll with it. In your organization, strategies will be planned, announced, implemented, and then — right in the middle of execution — they will all too often have to be altered or aborted because of external changes. What leaders need from employees is the ability to commit to a course of action and, *at the same time,* to stay flexible enough to alter behavior and attitude quickly to support a new direction.

Leadership Strategy —
Help People Control Stress

The pressures of business require the ability to manipulate daily stress levels. Many people thrive on stress, in manageable amounts. To these people, stress lends zest to life. "Eustress" is the term coined to label a positive level of stress that heightens productivity, creativity and enjoyment of life.

Stress is basically a response, a flow of energy if you will. A certain amount of stress is necessary for top performance. (The only truly stress-free people are dead.) So, up to a point, stress increases motivation and productivity. When the stress level continues to rise above that point, however, it becomes *dis*tress and negative consequences begin to take effect. Ill effects of negative stress include high blood pressure, headaches, chronic muscle tension, and the general weakening of the immune system. When you are in this mode a great deal of the time your brain stops functioning well and your judgement is clouded. Chronic stress is also linked to short-term memory loss and poor decision-making. Change-adept achievers have learned how to manipulate stress levels — to generate the right amount of eustress which for them assures optimal performance — and to utilize stress-reduction techniques when they begin to go into stress overload.

Distress is the chronic, unabated triggering of the stress response without intervening discharge. Bad stress can also be triggered by feelings that one's decisions are useless, that life is out of control. In fact, research shows that the most detrimental work situation is one in which high stress — increased work load — combines with low control over and at what rate the work is accomplished.

A simple stress-control technique that organizations can implement emphasizes the importance of giving employees autonomy over their work breaks. Studies within the California State University system and elsewhere have shown that employees who are encouraged to take voluntary breaks from tough assignments will outperform those who are denied that freedom. The form of the break is not important, although a complete disengagement from the task seems to be most beneficial. Some employees close their eyes and take deep breaths, some get a cup of coffee, others take a walk or do crossword puzzles. The pertinent factor is that employees are in control of the timing of their schedule and the content of their breaks.

Leadership Strategy —
Don't Make Everything a Crisis

Dean Tjosvold, professor of organizational behavior at Simon Fraser University's School of Business Administration, found that problem solvers worked most constructively when confronted with serious, but not critical issues. At moderate stress levels, he discovered, people are more apt to weigh alternatives, solicit opposing points of view, and invite constructive controversy in the problem-solving process.

When faced with a full-blown crisis, however, even experienced professionals can slip, grasp for quick-fix solutions, or take the path of least resistance — anything to bring an end to the emotional turmoil of high stress levels. Similarly, people dealing with problems they perceive as minor do not put forth their best efforts. Under low-stress conditions, the temptation is to ignore the problem or apply pat solutions. What is clear, according to Tjosvold, is that too much stress or too little stress can stymie effective decision-making, while moderate amounts of stress can actually facilitate it.

Some leaders wrongly believe that a "crisis mentality" is necessary to keep a workforce from becoming complacent, so these leaders constantly refer to any current situation as disastrous. Keeping a workforce in a state of constant crisis is difficult to justify as an effective management strategy: either employees stop believing that things are as bad as they're being presented (thereby making the organization more vulnerable to a genuine crisis) or they push themselves to respond in a high-stress mode and the organization suffers from employee burn-out and inadequate problem solving.

On the other hand, leaders who give employees a well-rounded picture of industry trends, competitive pressures, and customer demands help workers approach business challenges with a realistic idea of the amount of stress needed to do the best job. Don't use crisis as a motivating tactic. It's counterproductive. Be honest. Keep communication channels open and trust employees to respond appropriately to difficult situations. When a real crisis does strike they'll come through for you — if they've been treated responsibly.

Leadership Strategy —
Lighten Up

A sense of humor and fun are requisites for a change-adept workplace. Leaders should encourage others to lighten up. As the president of a title insurance company said to me, "To survive in this business, you'd better have a sense of humor." He's not alone in his assessment. Robert Half International surveyed vice presidents and human resource directors of 100 large companies. Some 84 percent of those interviewed thought that people with a sense of humor do a better job than people with little or no humor. Employees who could laugh and have fun were most likely to be creative and flexible.

Change offers plenty of reasons to be upset, worried and confused. A manager at a manufacturing plant going through its third restructuring in as many years said to me: "Things are often so emotional around here that I could laugh or I could cry. Crying may be soothing, but laughter is healing."

Laughter is also a natural tension reducer. Dr. William Fry of Stanford University refers to laughter as "internal jogging." In times of high stress, laughter distracts attention and stimulates the brain to release endorphins, the body's natural morphine-like substance. As laughter subsides, muscles of the body go limp, and the benefits of this relaxation last up to 45 minutes.

The playful side of our adult nature has always taken a back seat to the exercise of rational thought. In organizational settings, we have been conditioned to suppress our playful minds and to be serious about business. But lately, some leaders are finding tremendous benefit in developing flexible employees through fun and even play. According to research at the University of Alabama, managers who were accepted as friends by employees engaged in the humor network in the same proportion as other members of the team. In other words, when managers initiate jokes and are the target of jokes as much as anyone else, subordinates regard them as colleagues rather than just bosses.

Many organizations consciously make *fun* an integral part of the business. But when it comes to projecting an image of fun verging on lunacy — and making that image pay off — there is no better example than Southwest Airlines. In their book *Nuts! Southwest Airlines' Crazy Recipe for Business and Personal Success*, authors Kevin and Jackie Freiberg offer an example of corporate silliness at its zenith in their account of the "Malice in Dallas" arm-wrestling tournament between Herb Kelleher, then CEO of Southwest, and Kurt Herwald, the chairman of Stevens Aviation. In the Dallas Sportatorium, before a crowd of employees and the media, Kelleher and Herwald arm-wrestled to decide the user rights to a particular slogan. Rather than engage in a drawn-out, costly legal battle, the executives had chosen to decide the issue with the best two out of three matches.

The Freibergs set the scene: "The restless murmur of the crowd, punctuated by the shouts and chants of cheerleaders, crescendoed quickly to hoarse shouts and piercing whistles as, from the darkness at the top of the aisles, the two contenders marched toward the ring. Down one aisle strode Herwald, a burly 37-year-old weight lifter, dressed in slacks and a dark-colored muscle shirt, wearing a menacing sneer and displaying the tattoo 'Born to Raise Capital' on his massive right arm. Down the other, to the hair-raising trumpet blasts of the theme from Rocky, strutted the skinny, white-haired, 61-year-old Kelleher decked out in a white T-shirt, gray sweat pants under shiny red boxing shorts, a sling on his right arm and a cigarette dangling from his infectious grin, accompanied by a handler wearing a bandolera holding rows of airline-size bottles of Wild Turkey."

Kelleher lost the match, blaming a fractured wrist (injured, he claimed, while saving a little girl from being hit by a bus) combined with a week-long cold, a stubborn case of athlete's foot, and having accidentally overtrained by walking up a flight of steps. Herwald announced shortly after his victory that he had decided to let Southwest keep using the slogan "Just Plane Smart," and the story became another symbol of the company's zany, irreverent style.

Factor #4 — Counterbalance

One definition of the word compensate is "to provide with a counterbalance or neutralizing device." Change-adept individuals compensate for the demands and pressures of business by developing counterbalancing activities in other areas of their lives. They engage in exercise programs and healthful eating habits, they cultivate interests outside of business — sports, hobbies, art, music, etc. — that are personally fulfilling, and they have sources of emotional support. Because employees with counterbalance have a life that includes both work and recreation, they handle stress better and are more effective on the job. Most of all, they have an external source of stability which many refer to as their "anchor" or "rock."

One of the most memorable interviews I conducted on this topic was with the CEO of a cellular telephone company: "I've got one of those 'anchors' in my life. It's my sock drawer." I must have looked startled because he continued quickly. "I mean it," he said. "All hell can be breaking loose at work, but when I come home at night I open my sock drawer to find everything in color-coded, neat little piles. I tell you, it does my heart good."

I've included this story in my speeches for years, and only once have I had someone take offense at it. I had addressed the national convention of a real estate firm in Florida. A sales manager from California came up to me after the speech and wanted to book a similar program for his division. "I really enjoyed your talk," he said. "But when you speak to my group, please don't make fun of the sock drawer."

I told the sales manager that I would be happy to do as he asked, but was curious about the reason for his request. He looked at me sternly. "I don't want you to make fun of it because *it works*. I tell all of my sales people that if they are having a terrible day, where nothing is going right, they might as well go home and straighten out their underwear drawer."

He's right. It doesn't matter if the source of counterbalance sounds silly to others; change-adept people know what works for them.

Leadership Strategy —
Encourage Employees to Work as if Life Mattered

During one of AT&T's many transformations, I interviewed the woman in charge of Employee Health Services to find out what she'd observed about the most resilient people in the organization. I asked her if she noticed anything that resilient people had in common: Were they employed in a particular geographic region? Had they reached a certain level of the hierarchy? Did they perform similar functions? Were they male or female?

The manager told me that none of those factors made a difference. She said, "People who handle change best in this organization have two things in common: They take good care of themselves and they have outside interests."

As I continued talking with change-adept employees, the same themes kept repeating in my interviews. Those who are most resilient not only have a job — they have a life. Leaders develop change-adept workers when they understand and support the idea of balancing work and life. A successful executive passed on this advice to his staff: "Do not sacrifice your health or your family for any company. Even if the organization treats you extremely well, as it has treated me, it is still not worth trading a life for a career."

Leadership Strategy —
Encourage Counterbalance for the Brain

In 1981, Roger Sperry won the Nobel prize for his research with split brain theory. When Sperry surgically severed the corpus callosum connecting the left and right hemispheres of the brain, his studies showed that the two sides of the brain performed different functions.

The right and left hemispheres each specialize in distinct types of thinking processes. With 95 percent of all right-handed people, the left side of the brain not only cross-controls the right side of the body, but is also responsible for analytical, linear, verbal and rational thought. When you add columns of numbers, remember names and dates, and set goals and objectives, you are using your left brain. The right brain hemisphere controls the left side of the body and carries out holistic, imaginative, nonverbal and artistic functions. When you recall someone's face, become engrossed in a symphony, or daydream, you are engaging right-brain functions.

A young man once asked management expert Peter Drucker how to become a better manager. "Learn to play the violin," Drucker replied. Activities that stimulate the right side of the brain — whether playing a musical instrument, painting pictures, or ballroom dancing — provide counterbalance to an over-reliance on left-brain abilities.

Leaders who encourage employees to develop talents (which have nothing to do with their jobs) find there are unexpected business benefits. The president of CalTex in Kuala Lumpur told me that his company pays for any kind of educational course that employees want to take — the only exceptions being martial arts and cooking classes. He said that the most popular course is singing lessons. This was not totally unexpected since Malaysian employees regularly frequent karaoke bars after work. What he didn't anticipate, however, was the degree to which employees' singing lessons improved their ability in giving business-related presentations. People conquered stage fright and became comfortable with standing in front of groups. In fact, the only complaint from the president of the company was, "Now they think they can sing!"

Factor #5 — Creativity

Buckminster Fuller once said, "Everyone is born a genius. Society de-geniuses them." Change-adept professionals have survived the de-geniusing by society to remain curious, creative, and innovative. You can easily spot creative people in organizations. They are the employees who are constantly seeking ways to improve products, services, or themselves. Typically, they questions rules and regulations, and contribute ideas beyond the limits of their job descriptions — to other functions, to other departments, and to the organization as a whole. These creative employees solicit diverse opinions that generate new thoughts, and they value any business experience that exposes them to new knowledge and skills. One project manager summed it up when he said, "If this venture fails, it will still be worth all the time and effort I've put into it for the past 18 months. Just look at everything I've learned!"

Leadership Strategy —
Harness the Collective Genius

There was a time when popular opinion held that only a few departments in an organization housed creative people — usually corporate communications, public relations, research and development, and marketing. In the old framework, only top executives were expected to solve problems and develop new concepts. Such a limited view not only placed an enormous burden on the "creative few" to come up with all the answers, it also restricted the contributions of workers most knowledgeable about the problem situation.

Creativity is a set of skills that can be developed and applied daily at all levels throughout the organization. A factory peopled by unskilled laborers can benefit from innovative solutions just as much as the most high-powered think tank. For example, a factory employee at Period Furniture, a manufacturing company in Kentucky, devised a solution to problems caused by screws on the plant floor. By installing magnets on the bottoms of all company vehicles, the safety problems and flat tires caused by the dropped screws were eliminated.

Unleashing the innovative potential in a workforce comes only when leadership recognizes the natural creativity that exists within everyone and is willing to remove the tight barriers that have restricted the flow of creative ideas. Here's how to begin:

• **Make creativity a part of all job descriptions.**
Studies show that the biggest stumbling block to employee creativity at work is the perceived discouragement by management of such activity. You want to lead an organization to greater heights of creative innovation? Then make it clear that you need, expect, and value creative input from everybody.

• **Gather employee suggestions in "idea campaigns."**
The best programs are short-term (one or two months), focus

on a single issue (improving safety, cutting costs, eliminating paper-work, delighting customers), and are kept lively and fun ("Sacred Cow" hunts to question traditional methods, "Burn the Books" campaigns to reduce organizational rules and procedures).

- **Offer courses in creative problem solving for all employees — not just managers or "creative types."**
A study at the University of Buffalo found that employees who have been trained in creative thinking techniques generate twice as many suggestions than untrained employees.

- **Encourage the cross-pollination of ideas.**
At 3M, managers regularly organize internal "trade shows" that let different departments share one another's brainstorms and innovations. The result at 3M is a perpetual state of creative competition within the company.

- **Stimulate ideas by taking a field trip.**
IDEO is one of the largest and most innovative industrial product design firms in the world. Designers at IDEO visit the local hardware store to see new products and remind themselves of old ideas, and they take field trips to places such as the Barbie Hall of Fame, an airplane junkyard, and a competition where custom-built robots fight to the death.

- **Give employees the freedom to be creative.**
American Greeting Cards sent a team of its artists to a camp-site in the woods — away from the eyes of management — to invent characters that can be used in toys, movies and comic books. This is a big change from the days when bosses gave the company artists ideas to work on, and the artists were confined to their individual cubicles at corporate headquarters.

• **Reward innovations with private and public recognition.**

And if the idea is especially valuable, reward its creator with a cash bonus, royalties or a percentage of the profits generated by the idea. At ICI Pharmaceuticals Group in Wilmington, Delaware, the Performance Excellence Award is given to employees for any idea that helps the business (saving money, increasing productivity, etc.) or to employees who go "above and beyond" the call of duty. The award winner receives $300. A person can be nominated for this award by anyone: a peer, supervisor, coworker or department head.

Leadership Strategy —
Understand the Creative Process

The concept that creativity follows a particular pattern was popularized by Graham Wallace in *The Art of Thought.* In his book, Wallace proposed the following four-step process that should be taught to everyone from whom you expect creative contributions:

Preparation — In the first part of the creative process, a clear understanding of the situation is established. I refer to this first step as "doing your homework." Creativity does not take the place of logical and strategic thinking — it merely supplements it. Initially, you need to gather all the relevant data, talk to others to broaden your perspective, find out what has been tried in the past, and get a sense of the emotions that are embedded in the situation. In a corporate setting, it is also crucial that you consider the importance of this challenge in meeting the goals and supporting the values of the organization.

Incubation — Once the situation has been thoroughly defined, the next step is to divert your attention and release the problem from conscious thought. Diverting attention from the problem situation allows the subconscious mind to synthesize and make connections in holistic and intuitive ways that supersede sole reliance on logic.

Illumination — Illumination is the stage in which you feel a sudden burst of knowledge. The subconscious alerts the conscious through an "ah-ha" experience in which images, thoughts or understandings break through to awareness.

Verification — The final step is a "reality check." Is the idea practical, cost-effective and timely? Can you explain it convincingly? Where can you test it? Can you rally support? What are the most likely objections to be raised by critics? How will you answer the objections?

Leadership Strategy —
Look for Multiple Right Answers

In the Information Age, ideas become *the* strategic edge for organizations. Innovation and creativity are quickly becoming the keys to corporate productivity and excellence. Never before has it been so crucial for a workforce to generate new ideas.

Two-time Nobel prize winner Linus Pauling said, "The best way to get good ideas is to begin with lots of ideas." On an airplane trip from San Francisco to Toronto, I sat next to Dr. Pauling. When I asked him about the greatest obstacle to generating a multitude of ideas, he replied that it was "any process — educational, scientific, or organizational — that insists on a single right answer."

In today's business world, we are dealing with complex challenges that defy overly simple or one-right-answer solutions. Today there are multiple right answers: a system that works in one department may not be appropriate company-wide; successful management approaches in the United States may not work in overseas centers; and leadership skills are most effective when they are situational — adapted to fit different people and circumstances. Continuous improvement is the process by which current right ways constantly transform to become even more effective. As I tell my audiences: "Just remember — there is always more than one right way to deliver pizza, babies, or a joke."

Leaders help employees generate lots of ideas when they ask these kinds of questions:

- **How would we do it now if we had never done it before?**
If we were starting this business from scratch, what are the first things you would do differently? If you could write a new job description, how would you redesign your job?

What questions do your kids ask you about work that you can't answer? If you were new to the organization, what questions would you ask?

- **What are a variety of perspectives about this situation?**
How does this problem look through the eyes of our customers — suppliers — competitors — the community — people in different departments of the company — people in different cultures?

What are our assumptions about this situation? (Write them down and then write the opposites. Analyze what would happen if the opposite assumptions proved correct.)

- **Which organizational rules are best broken?**
Analyze each rule and traditional business practice: What are we doing? Why did we start doing it? Does it still need to be done that way? What would happen if we stopped doing it? What are some better ways of doing it?

- **That's one right answer. What's another?**
Help employees move from looking for a single solution to

multiple possibilities by embracing the philosophy that there is more than one right way to do business.

Leadership Strategy —
Respect Intuition

When Jonas Salk became a scientist, he would picture himself as a virus or a cancer cell and try to sense what it would be like to be either. I asked Linus Pauling (it was a long flight) about the value of intuition and he told me that he had once struggled for months with a problem in chemistry that caught his interest — the reason why a certain kind of anesthesia worked. Seven years later, while walking down the street thinking of nothing except what a pleasant day it was, the answer popped into his head fully formed. "Something finally triggered it," he said. "You have to learn to trust your intuition, even if it takes seven years."

Andrew Carnegie, John D. Rockefeller, and Conrad Hilton are examples of executives who were known for their intuitive business decisions. A story about Conrad Hilton highlights the value of what was referred to as "Connie's hunches." There was to be a sealed bid on a New York property. Hilton evaluated its worth at $159,000 and prepared a bid in that amount. He slept that night and upon awakening, the figure $174,000 stood out in his mind. He changed the bid and submitted the higher figure. It won. The next highest bid was $173,000. Hilton subsequently sold the property for several million dollars.

Traditionally, American employees have been schooled to be logical. They are told to rely on numbers and data-collection techniques to solve problems, and so shy away from intuitive approaches that might be more appropriate. In times of rapid change, analysis is often too slow a tool for decision-making. Frequently it is the hunch that defies logic, the "gut feeling" or the flash of insight that turns out to be the best solution.

Intuition is what you add to the information you collect. If you understand that, you see you can never collect total information. You have to add your feelings and your gut reaction to make good decisions. In that sense, there is no answer that is right for everybody — just what's right for you. A workforce that is both highly cognitive and highly intuitive has a distinct advantage in achieving innovative results. Leaders help people in the organization go beyond a purely logical approach to problem solving by acknowledging the validity of emotion, imagination and intuition.

Leadership Strategy —
Entertain Outrageous Ideas

I was hired to facilitate a problem-solving session for a group of 94 male technical workers, none of whom had had previous training in creative thinking. We spent the morning "warming up" with creativity techniques, and in the afternoon the group was divided into teams for brainstorming sessions. By the end of the day, each team was to present their ideas to their boss, and he in turn would give authorization and funds to implement the best solutions.

The morning had gone well when we were all together, but this "creative stuff" was new to everyone, and I was afraid that the isolated teams would revert to the (safer) tried-and-true solutions of the past. To prevent that from happening, I gave a last set of instructions to the group. I reminded them to follow the rules of classical brainstorming:

- Write all ideas on a large sheet of paper or chalkboard so that everyone can see.
- Aim initially for quantity, not quality of ideas.
- "Piggy-back" on the ideas of others, adding some new twist to the original suggestions.
- Hold off judgements and critical evaluation until after all ideas are collected.

Then I added an extra item to the list of instructions. I asked them to spend the final five minutes thinking of things that would absolutely work — but were too expensive, illegal, or in some other way, too ridiculous to consider.

When the teams reassembled to present their solutions to the group vice president, each team leader said the same thing: "This started out as our most ridiculous idea, but the more we thought about it, the more it appealed to us. So we found ways to make it our best practical solution."

It is possible to find practical potential in the most outrageous possibilities, but that won't happen in your organization unless leadership is willing to entertain wild ideas in the first place.

Leadership Strategy —
Encourage Diversity of Opinion

If you and I are in a problem-solving session and we think exactly alike, one of us is redundant. An exercise I have used to make this point is a grid of 16 "brainteaser" puzzles. I allow five minutes for people to try to solve the puzzles by themselves, and then I put them into teams to finish the exercise. Before they begin to work together I ask, "What is it that you want from the other team members?" Without fail, the answer comes back: "I want the solutions that I don't already have."

Conformity is the antithesis of creative collaboration. Conformity is what the training film *Brain Power* refers to as "collective ignorance." Creative collaboration, in contrast, is the process of blending diverse opinion, expertise, and perspective toward a shared objective. There are many advantages to a diversified employee base, and increased creativity is high on the list. We need the perspectives, insights and solutions from people who do not think exactly like we do. We need the answers we don't already have. We need creative collaboration. Leaders demonstrate their belief in diversity when they invite various points of view and utilize the ideas and suggestions of others.

Leadership Strategy —
Nurture Suggestions and Ideas

An employee at Eli Lilly & Co. suggested a way to recover and reuse the expensive chemical tetrahydrofuran instead of disposing of it as waste, saving the company $708,787 in the recovery program's first year. IBM used an employee suggestion for a tool to mold special computer cable and saved $1.4 million in the first year after inception. A loan manager at Bank of America saved the bank an estimated $363,520 a year just by discovering that there was no need to pay $50 per home loan for property-tax information that could be obtained for free.

What's one idea worth to your organization? Maybe millions? What's the value of harnessing the creative capacity of an entire workforce? In a single year at Japan Mazda, 27,000 employees generated 2.7 million suggestions for improvement — an average of 100 ideas from each worker. The company implemented 82 percent of these ideas.

Ideas are elusive and fragile. Those who want to increase the creativity of a workforce need to ask this most important question: How are new ideas treated?

It is easy to discourage creativity by responding to new ideas with such phrases as, "We tried it before," "We don't do it that way here," "That's not your job," "We never tried that before, so it's too risky," "Our place is different," or "It's against company policy."

If you judge an idea too soon you won't see its full potential. Ideas take time and care to mature. Developing a safe haven for ideas takes a willingness to let ideas emerge freely and to be receptive to them. Nurturing creativity means curbing indifference and harsh criticism so that employees feel free to ask "dumb" questions, challenge rules, and offer novel suggestions.

Leaders who nurture creativity do so by building a relaxed, informal work environment, where rules are de-emphasized, employees are encouraged to mix and mingle, and people feel safe in sharing their inspirations with others. Idea-promoters respond to new ideas with comments like: "Is this what you meant?" "I appreciate your input." "I don't know if we can do all of it, but I very much like this part of your idea."

Factor #6: Collaboration

Human beings thrive in collaborative relationships. Given the right context, they can do great things together. Connect just two of us, working in concert, and you get the X-ray, or the airplane — or the comic genius of Laurel and Hardy. Hook up 20 of us, as the British did in WWII, and you crack the German military code. A new workplace reality — and one that is driving collaboration and teamwork throughout our organizations — is that none of us can succeed alone. Success in the future will increasingly depend on how well we collaborate to find innovative solutions to organizational problems. This process can be as personally gratifying as it is organizationally profitable. As one change-adept professional said, "There is a phenomenal sense of accomplishment in achieving as a group what could not have been achieved as individuals."

Leadership Strategy —
Calculate the High Cost of Lost Knowledge

In the perfect collaborative model, managers are valued not because they know more than their staffs, but because they can quickly communicate to their staffs what they know and get staff members to do the same with each other. Leaders build environments of trust and mutual respect where creative contribution is nurtured, and where employees at all levels understand that being successful in this networked world increasingly requires collaboration and knowledge-sharing.

That's the ideal. The reality is somewhat different. I recently surveyed managers about the state of collaboration in their companies. I found that, all too often: bosses withhold information and dole it out on a "need to know" basis, executives ask for collaborative input when what they really want is a "rubber stamp" for decisions already made, and people aren't sharing what they know due to a variety of personal and organizational inhibitors.

This is an extremely expensive set of circumstances. International Data Corporation developed a metric to measure what they refer to as the "knowledge deficit." It captures the costs and inefficiencies that result from intellectual rework, substandard performance and the inability to find knowledge resources. According to this metric, the knowledge deficit among Fortune 500 companies costs them, conservatively, $12 billion annually.

In addition to that, best practices and lessons learned have the potential to save companies billions of dollars more. Kenneth Derr, the former Chief Executive Officer of Chevron, saw the situation this way: "Every day that a better idea goes unused is a lost opportunity. We have to share more, and we have to share faster. I tell employees that sharing and using best practices is the single most important thing they can do."

Leadership Strategy –
Understand Why People Don't Readily Share Knowledge

There are many reasons why people are reluctant to share what they know. They are busy and don't have time to share. They forget to share. They don't want the additional work and responsibility that goes with sharing. They are assigned to projects they feel are unworthy of their contribution (a derisive term for this kind of project is WOMBAT—waste of money, brains and time). And in this post-Enron environment, there is a general reluctance to trust in the credibility of senior management. But, as common as these conditions may be, they were not the responses given most often in my research.

Here are the top five reasons why people don't tell what they know:

1. People believe that knowledge is power.
   "If I know something you don't know, I have something over you."
   (These quotes are from managers in my study.)
2. People are insecure about the value of their knowledge.
   "I feel that people tend to underestimate life experience, that intellect has been so overpraised, and for some people without a formal education, that it is hard for them to believe that they can add value in a very different way."
3. People don't trust each other.
   "I didn't know the other members of the team personally, so I didn't trust them."
4. Employees are afraid of negative consequences.
   "I was afraid that my idea would be ridiculed if it were slightly 'over the top,' rather than looked at as a useful brainstorming point."
5. People work for other people who don't tell what they know.
   "Personally, I have had more problems with managers and decision makers withholding information than I have had with colleagues or team members."

(If you are interested in learning more about this topic, my book, *GHOST STORY: A Modern Business Fable,* is an entertaining tale about why people don't share knowledge. You can preview it at: www.CKG.com.)

Leadership Strategy —
Create a Climate for Collaboration

Educational systems are designed to discourage information-sharing. If I give you an answer to a question on a test, and we are graded on a curve, I have put myself at a disadvantage. Most people still struggle with the idea that if they tell you what they know, they'll lose something. When a company's evaluation, promotion and compensation are based on relative numbers, the perception is that sharing knowledge will (always) reduce the chance of personal success.

Therefore, the first obvious step in creating a climate that encourages collaboration is to change the reward system. Find ways to reinforce and reward collaboration. Recognize and promote people who learn, teach and share. And penalize those who do not. In all best-practices companies, hoarding knowledge and failing to build on ideas of others have visible and sometimes serious career consequences. At American Management Systems, "leveraging" what you know by educating colleagues, writing, helping others and teaching junior staff is how you build your reputation as a world-class thought leader and how you get promoted to partner. To reinforce collaboration at Buckman Laboratories, Bob Buckman's policy was that the people who engage in active and effective knowledge-sharing would be the *only* ones considered for promotion.

Second, understand that there are more powerful motivators than money. For 25,000 Xerox field service technicians around the world, contributing to the Eureka database of maintenance tips is an opportunity to become known as a thought leader. To be personally identified with the solution to a difficult problem, in front of Xerox service reps all over the world, is the biggest incentive in getting people to contribute. At Xerox, they demonstrate that knowledge-hoarding is no longer power, but a reputation for knowledge-sharing is.

Third, give staff access to information. In any organization, the way information is handled determines whether it becomes an obstacle to or an enabler of knowledge-sharing. In the Industrial Age, information management was deliberately obstructive as a matter of policy. Employees weren't expected to contribute to decision-making or problem-solving, so the information they were given was restricted to the bare minimum management felt they needed to do their own particular jobs.

Today, informed collaboration is seen as essential for organizational success, and leaders need to make sure that every employee has access to every fact about every aspect of the business—terrifying or not—including finances, competitive products/services and organizational strategy. Moreover, this calls for an increased investment in educational and personal development programs so that all employees have enough practical background to utilize the business data being shared.

Leadership Strategy —
Optimize the Power of "Mini-Cultures"

There are mini-cultures in every organization. Regardless of the overall corporate culture, individual managers and team leaders can nurture a climate for collaboration within their own work group or staff. And the best of these leaders do so by taking the time and effort necessary to make people feel safe and valued. They emphasize people's strengths while encouraging the sharing of mistakes and lessons learned. They set clear expectations for outcomes and clarify individual roles. They help all members recognize what each of them brings to the team. They model openness, vulnerability and honesty. They tell stories of group successes and personal challenges. And most of all, they encourage and respect everyone's contribution. While no one can command others to collaborate and share knowledge, leaders can influence people to do so by creating an environment in which it is safe, enjoyable and beneficial to do so.

Leadership Strategy —
Build Trust

A culture for collaboration must be based on trust. Yet, too often, in the rush to get started on a new project, we get groups of people together and tell them to "get to work." This approach proves less than productive, as the group hasn't had time to discover each other's strengths and weakness nor to develop a common understanding and vision for the project. In addition, high turnover, mass layoffs and early retirements make it extremely challenging to develop the mutual trust necessary to build strong relationships throughout the organization.

Since people are naturally reluctant to collaborate with others when they don't know them well enough, the solution begins with creating opportunities for people to meet and interact in both formal and informal settings. And don't rush them. Give people time to develop relationships, to evaluate each other's trustworthiness, and to learn each other's strengths and weaknesses well enough to adapt constructively to them. Taking time to build this "social capital" at the beginning of a project increases the effectiveness of the team later on.

Even the motivation for individuals to contribute knowledge to an electronic data base is largely dependent on the relationship of the members who use the system. If individuals do not trust others with their knowledge, or don't trust that others will contribute in kind, it is unlikely that the system will be effective. Technology can facilitate collaboration, but it is trust that enables it.

And remember: Trusting is not a matter of blind deference, but of placing — or refusing to place — trust with good judgement. Trust is fragile, and building it isn't easy. There's no quick fix. Built slowly over time, it grows as people take small risks and wait for those acts of faith to be justified and reciprocated. And, unless there are reserves of trust, it can be destroyed overnight. The good news is that when trust is pervasive it becomes the force that energizes teammates, releases creative contribution and makes working together both productive and a joy.

Many years ago, a renowned European chess grandmaster played an exhibition match against a New York amateur — and lost. The champion was celebrated for his chessboard strategy — for his ability to plan a dozen or more moves ahead as a game developed — and at the post-match press conference the amateur was asked how many moves ahead he had planned in defeating the master. "Only one," he replied. "The right one."

There, in a nutshell, lies the key to success in a constantly changing world. The amateur chess player wasn't talking about rigidity when he used the word "right." He was talking about flexible, creative reaction, about assessing each position as it developed on the board and then making the move that needed to be made at the moment. He did have an overall game plan, but he didn't frustrate himself trying to anticipate everything his opponent might do five or 20 moves hence. He knew he couldn't out-think the master. So keeping his basic plan in mind, he tailored his own moves to the immediate possibilities inherent in each position as it arose, and by sticking to that strategy he won a famous victory.

Which is exactly what the most successful leaders do today in response to the constantly shifting and always uncertain facts of life in the modern business world. They work out a general plan for the future, pin it up in the corners of their minds and then focus on what's happening right now. They assess all the possibilities inherent in each developing situation, decide what needs to be done and then make the move that will be most advantageous to their company's prosperity and ongoing strength within the parameters of the larger scheme. Sometimes the move will be an offensive, attacking one. Sometimes it will be a tactical side step. Sometimes it will be an unexpected counter-thrust. But whatever its character and consequence, it will be based on the best analysis of immediate circumstances, and it will be made in the knowledge that it may well affect the shape of the overall plan to some extent. Because every business strategy, like every chess game, is fraught with imponderables. Each position has its own unique possibilities and each opponent has his or her own ideas about how to capitalize on them.

Flexibility, open-mindedness, the capacity to roll with changing circumstances, the ability to absorb and assess new information and to apply it creatively to new situations — those are the strengths of the winning, change-adept company today. As Grandmaster Fred Reinfeld said in *Why You Lose At Chess* (a book every aspiring business leader would do well to study): "You lose because you're stubborn. You have prejudices and preconceived notions — and you refuse to give them up." Unforgivable, Reinfeld concludes. And doubly so in business where there is a good deal more to be lost than just a game.

But as a leader of a team or an organization, you have one enormous advantage over the chess player sitting alone at the board. All of your chess pieces can think, too. Even the pawns have great ideas to contribute. Listen to them. Don't feel threatened or take offense if someone else's ideas prove to be more effective than your own. It's the ideas that count, not who came up with them. Find ways to improve your team's self-confidence and sense of worth.

Help them to discover what's positive in challenging situations and how to cope constructively with change. Think about three-dimensional communication — about information that moves simultaneously up, down and across all layers of your organization with equal facility and openness. Forget about the leadership model that made you successful in the past. Shared knowledge and shared responsibility are what make businesses work today. Forget about the map on the candy box lid and pass the candy around instead, so that everyone can get a taste of what's there.

4

LEADING CHANGE

"How are we changing, why are we changing, and what's in it for me?"

"When there's a business challenge, you bring people together to identify the problem, and you jointly develop a solution. It may take a little more time to do that, but it really sustains the change, because people are engaged, energized and involved."

**Sue Swenson, President and Chief
Operation Officer, Leap Wireless**

THERE ARE TWO KINDS OF CHANGE — incremental and discontinuous — that are taking place simultaneously and constantly in all business organizations. Incremental change is the process of continuous improvement — what the Japanese refer to as "kaizen." Discontinuous change is the kind of large-scale transformation that turns the organization inside out and upside down. If managing incremental change can be compared to encouraging a group of joggers to gradually pick up the pace, then leading discontinuous change is like urging people to leap off a cliff and build their parachutes on the way down. It is no wonder that you can manage linear change, but you have to lead discontinuous change.

Incremental change fits the Newtonian framework of linear, progressive and predictable change. It uses current practices as a baseline for the systematic improvement of a product, service or system. There is an unmistakable logic behind incremental change that makes it easy to predict, easy to communicate and relatively easy for people to adopt. But much of the change our organizations are facing today is not incremental. It is transformative.

While most leaders are comfortable (and effective) managing incremental change, they are less than effective leading discontinuous organizational transformation. Part of the reason is that discontinuous change — restructuring, reengineering, transformation — challenges our most deeply held beliefs about company wellbeing. It confronts the entire organization with the possibility that the very roles, actions and attitudes that were *most* responsible for past success will be insufficient, and perhaps even detrimental, to success in the future. Discontinuous change challenges people at all levels of the organization to take on new roles, new relationships, new values and radically new approaches to their jobs. (Don't tell people "It's just business." This kind of change is personal.) But beyond the sheer magnitude of the change itself, and beyond management's often clumsy handling of the "human side" of the process, another overriding reason for the ineffectiveness of large-scale change efforts is that leaders are trying to manage discontinuity with the same linear approach they use with incremental change. And that just doesn't work.

WHY TRANSFORMATION FAILS

"I wasn't smart enough about people.
I was reflecting my engineering background and was
insufficiently appreciative of the human dimension.
I've learned that's critical."
Michael Hammer, *Reengineering the Corporation*

Most large-scale change efforts do not achieve their business objectives. A decade ago, the Wyatt Company conducted a study on why corporate restructuring fails so often. The findings concluded that failure occurred for one or a combination of the following reasons:

Employee resistance to change 58%
Dysfunctional corporate culture...............................43%
Inadequate management skills 37%
Lack of line management support...................................35%
Poor employee communication effort 26%
Lack of senior management visibility..............................21%
Intervention by outside forces (acts of God) 17%
Use of the wrong solution/approach 13%

Only the last item reflects poor strategy and analysis. Restructuring does not usually fail because of poor strategy. The top six reasons are all people issues, and yet most managers still don't understand the human side of the equation.

It is not that leaders are unaware of the problem. When asked to name the most important skill they need to succeed in the future, leaders almost universally put "managing change" at the top of their lists. It is just that the human aspect — the critical success factor in change-management — hasn't been adequately addressed. Consequently, most leaders are still trying to "sell" corporate transformation to employees who are increasingly unwilling to "buy" into it. Traditional methods of strategic planning by a concentrated group of executives don't provide the diverse perspectives and global views for setting a new course. And today, there simply isn't time for the "top-down," "cascade," "roll out" communication campaigns of the past. Instead, you need to involve the organization's stakeholders in strategic decisions.

It is not surprising that so many change efforts are failures. Under a management that doesn't realize the need for larger segments at all levels to be involved in shaping strategic direction, or understand the importance of facilitating people's natural emotional reactions, even naturally change-adept employees will be less eager to embrace transformation.

Organizations don't change. People do — or they don't. If you are unable to galvanize people into action, all the planning, the analysis, the strategic prioritizing doesn't matter at all.

FROM ANSWERS TO QUESTIONS

To repeat: Mobilizing an organization to transform itself in order to thrive in new business environments cannot be managed with linear strategies. In fact, the best techniques for transformation are not found in *any* formal strategy. Instead, the most effective guidelines to leading discontinuous change *evolve* as leaders reflect on the answers to a series of questions:

Question #1: What is the employees' perspective?

One night at sea, the ship's captain saw what looked like the lights of another ship heading toward him. He had his signalman blink to the other ship: Change your course 10 degrees south. The reply came back: Change *your* course 10 degrees north. The ship's captain answered: I am a captain. Change your course 10 degrees south. The reply was: I am a signalman first class. Change your course 10 degrees north. This infuriated the captain, so he signaled back: I say change your course south immediately. I'm on a battleship! To which the reply came: And I say change your course north. I'm in a lighthouse.

Like the ship's captain, leaders of discontinuous change can't rely solely on their own points of view. To mobilize a workforce for transformation leaders must know what people in the organization are thinking, must encourage them to articulate their points of view and their concerns, and must be ready to respond to them sincerely. The first question that leaders should ask is: "What is the employees' perspective?" And don't rely on second-hand information or make assumptions about what you *think* employees think. *Ask* them — and keep asking them until they tell you.

The Employees' Perspective

- What are the complaints you hear most often from customers? (In what ways are we disappointing customers?)
- What are the compliments you hear most often from customers? (In what ways do we please or delight customers?)
- What do you read in the newspapers or hear on the news that concerns you about the future of this company? (What are the rumors/stories about our company or about the industry that worry you?)
- What organizational policies, procedures, or systems get in the way of your doing superior work? (If you could throw out rules that interfere with your performance, what rules would go?)
- What do you like most about working in this organization that you *wouldn't* want to change? (What do you brag about to your friends and family?)

- If we were the competition, how would we outdo ourselves? (What do you personally think about how our products/services compare in value with those of our competitors?)
- What could be done to make your job more exciting? (How would you redesign your job to make it more challenging?)
- What trends are going to affect the future of this organization? (What changes have you read about or experienced — in technology, social values, globalization, etc. — that you believe will impact your job or this organization?)
- What are you concerned that the leadership of this company might do?
- What are you concerned that the leadership of this company might *not* do?

Everyone in the organization has a special knowledge and sees different needs and opportunities from their particular vantage points. People on the front lines get feedback that comes from working closest to the customer. Technical specialists have early access to technological innovations, and marketers track social and demographic trends. Once you gather the collective insight of the workforce and give the entire organization access to it, you may find that the impetus for transformation already exists. And only after you have an understanding of the employees' perspective will you be able to think through this next series of strategic questions:

- In what ways does employee perception already align with yours? Are their views of customer reactions in line with yours? Do they see the same organizational strengths/weaknesses/challenges that you do? Are they also aware of the trends that you see as the most urgent for the organization? Is there a perception that jobs could be more rewarding with fewer rules — and is that your perspective as well?

- How can you build on this alignment when leading transformation? Just as in a negotiation, places of convergent agreement give you a foundation: "We all agree that the customer is disappointed with our speed of delivery." "Most of you think that new technologies are going to allow you to work at least part of the time from your home. I think so too." "Some of you are concerned about the temporary workforce we have hired lately. Here are my concerns." And so forth. Then, whatever you hear from employees, feed back to the entire workforce to let everyone know the collective understandings.

- Where are the gaps between your perception and theirs? What have employees reported that you haven't considered? Where is your perspective and vision out of alignment with theirs? If, for example, employees say they don't see the threat of international competition — and if this is an area of great importance in your view — you need to know early on that they won't accept competitive pressure as a reason for change unless they are given further evidence.

Question #2: Did you "set the stage" for change?

For a long time we've known that every company goes through a life cycle, from start-up to rapid growth, then into maturity and decline. What's new is that the cycle's time frame, which used to be 10 years or more, is now two years or even less. Jack Welch, the former CEO of General Electric, said that one of the hardest situations he faced was when employees ask, "Is the change finally over?" Welch had to look at those employees and reply, "No. It's only just begun." People need to know *why* they are being asked to change, and the earlier they understand the reason, the more time they have to get prepared. They also need to know why "change has only just begun." But the most crucial information people must have to prepare for the future is why the very nature of organizational change has gone from linear steps to discontinuous leaps. To prepare people to cope in today's nanosecond world, leaders must adopt a Living-Systems Model that explains discontinuous change as the *natural* process for organizations. Leaders must help the workforce look at transformation not as a threat, but as exciting, challenging and desirable. ·

In most organizations we "Braille the culture," as one professional trend spotter, Faith Popcorn, put it. We run our fingertips along trend bumps as they speed by and try to "read" where we're going. One of the most vital roles of leadership is to anticipate the corporation's future and its place in the global arena, and then to formulate strategies for surmounting challenges that have not yet manifested. To proactively respond to these challenges, businesses must continually reinvent themselves. Leaders must encourage employees to join a constant questioning of the prevailing business assumptions — and to be ready to act upon new opportunities early in the game to maintain a competitive advantage. And when competitors begin to catch up, organizations must be prepared to introduce new products and services that will make their current ones obsolete — even if they are currently successful. To keep in front of the market, organizations must be ready to reinvent themselves every day.

Effective leaders find ways to anticipate trends and ride the leading edge of change by dedicating themselves to continual experimentation. But leaders can't be the only proactive members of the organization. They have to alert everyone to changing market realities. When Rubbermaid held a product fair in its headquarters town, it displayed storage bins, kitchen items and other plastic housewares, each with a label that detailed what it cost to make and what it sold for. Sounds like a run-of-the-mill corporate event except for two things: the fair was open only to Rubbermaid employees and the products were not Rubbermaid's, but its competitors. Rubbermaid wanted its workers to see for themselves what they were competing against.

More and more leaders are recognizing the need to design and manage a workplace environment that enables people to experience for themselves the need for change. The key is to let employees discover the problem. You won't be successful if people aren't carrying the recognition of the problem and the solution within themselves.

The best time to discuss the forces of change is well in advance of the organization's response to them. Leaders develop proactive employees by teaching them to scan the business environment. Everyone in the organization should have a realistic appreciation of the precursors of organizational transformation — the impact of globalization, market fluctuations, technological innovations, societal and demographic changes in the customer base, new offerings by competitors, new government and regulatory decisions. Employees should also understand how their company, like any living system, thrives on the edge of chaos. Rather than protecting people from outside threats, leaders need to expose workers to the complaints of customers, the new products of international competitors, and the financial reality of costs and profits. Instead of stifling conflicting opinions, leaders must view conflict as the force that drives creativity and learning. To stimulate productive conflict, leaders need to engage the workforce in an ongoing dialogue about the most basic business assumptions:

- What business are we in?
- Why are we in business?
- Who are our customers?

- What do our customers want? (How do we know?)
- How and where do we best serve our customers? (How do we know?)
- Who is our competition?
- How does your current department/job add value to the organization?

When the rules of competition change, it can happen virtually overnight, and all organizations must stay alert to be able to respond quickly. Federal Express challenged the United States Post Office and changed the "rules" of package delivery, and Southwest became the most profitable U.S. airline by rewriting the "rules" about ticket pricing, turnaround time and what constitutes customer service.

Questions that stimulate strategic speculation include:

- What would happen if our current forms of distribution were inaccessible to us?
- What government regulations could "change the rules" of the industry?
- What social trends could cause our customers to stop buying our product or service?
- What kinds of technological innovation would most drastically affect our product or service?
- What changes (in pricing, services, process, etc.) could the competition introduce that would cause us to rethink the way we do business?
- What companies that aren't our competitors now could become competitors in the future?
- What current competitors could become partners in the future?
- What are the global trends that could most affect our market?

- Under what conditions could this industry become obsolete?

Question #3: Are you tracking employee perceptions throughout the change?

As important as it is to find out what employees are thinking before the change, it is just as crucial to have a system for monitoring employee perception throughout the change process. George Bernard Shaw once said that the problem with communication is "the illusion that it has been accomplished." When it comes to communicating change, leadership must be especially careful not to suffer that illusion.

Strategies that include employee interaction and feedback systems help organizations track the level of workforce comprehension. You will find the greatest advantages come when organizational feedback is gathered immediately after the delivery of every important message. One of my clients uses this short questionnaire to query her audiences before they leave the meeting room:

- What in your view are the most important points we just covered?
- What didn't you understand?
- With what do you disagree?
- With what do you agree?
- What else do you need to know?

Leaders at Kodak use CAT (Communication Advisory Teams) as both a sounding board for new communications and as a feedback system for the effectiveness of current communications. Chosen for their ability to speak up candidly, the members of CAT represent a vertical slice of the organization. Their primary function is to remark on the quality of communications: What are they hearing? What is their reaction to the message? What questions do they have? What would make the communication more effective? Although strictly a management option, another purpose that CAT can serve is as a preview audience for upcoming corporate presentations and announcements. Leaders can "audition" their speeches: "Here is what I want to talk about. What is your opinion of my style? How is this information going to make people feel?"

A similar communication strategy was developed by consultants at Watson Wyatt. Wyatt discovered that real communication takes place *after* the formal communication — the article in the employee newsletter, the boss's announcement, the video presentation by the CEO — when work group peers seek the reaction of colleagues whose opinions are most influential. Wyatt recommends identifying these peer opinion leaders (POL) early on, and involving them in the design of the communication process for specific issues. The object of this strategy is to immerse these influential peers in the details of the issue so that these "organic" leaders become a natural horizontal communication channel for organizational change.

Question #4: Are you convincing people that change is necessary in successful times?

There is a story about a frog placed in a pot of lukewarm water over a fire that gradually heated the water to boiling. Because the frog failed to notice the point at which the water became hot enough to kill it, it stayed in the pot and was cooked. The danger of organizational success is that, like the warm water, it can lull us into a comfortable complacency that dismisses the signals of threat.

Traditionally, organizations in North America have changed in response to crisis. Today our organizations are dealing with forces that are so dynamic and fast moving that to wait until there is proof of crisis is to respond far too late. The way that the accelerated pace of change drastically shortens response time was once explained to me in the following manner: If I was walking down the middle of a residential street and I saw a car coming at me from a couple blocks away, there would be plenty of time to get to the sidewalk, but if I were in a jet plane heading for another jet plane traveling at the speed of sound, even two miles wouldn't be far enough away to react in time to avert a collision.

In order to keep the workforce onboard in the transformation of a successful organization, a leader must provide direction and the rationale for change by identifying future challenges and clarifying business realities. Leaders of enterprises must be able to view business patterns as if they were looking down from a rooftop. Leaders should give employees a strong sense of history of the enterprise and what was especially good about its past, as well as a clear idea of the market forces at work today and the responsibility people must take in shaping the future of the enterprise. And, once again, the leader's role in this process must shift from supplying slick solutions to framing key questions and bringing critical issues into corporate conversations.

One of the most effective strategies to convince employees to change when times are good utilizes proactive problem-solving: "What are the future challenges that we need to begin preparing for today?" coupled with status quo risk-analysis: "What is the risk of trying to stay competitive in this dynamic business environment with the organizational status quo?" When these issues have been honestly addressed by management and employees, people in the organization can understand a basic reality — regardless of your current level of success, in volatile times the greatest risk of all is not to change.

Question #5: Are you giving honest answers to tough questions?

In a study of hundreds of workers, management professor Jim Kouzes asked: "What trait do you look for in a supervisor?" With incredible consistency, respondents gave first preference to honesty.

It is no coincidence that I also found openness and honesty reiterated as essential ingredients for communicating change. In the light of economic realities that offer little in the way of job security, employees must be able to rely on their employer to give them honest information that will allow them to make informed choices about their own jobs, careers and futures.

The need for candor starts even before a person is hired. A study of corporate recruitment practices by M.E. Scott, a recruitment consulting firm, found that the most effective practices are those which offer job-seekers candid, detailed, job-specific information. More than elaborate promises, applicants mainly want to know what it will be like to work at a company. It is important to portray job requirements accurately — both the positive and the negative aspects — to the candidate. An equally candid description of the organization's culture will help a prospective employee form realistic expectations, and will increase the likelihood that the person will feel satisfied once on the job. When employers share strategic objectives, even new recruits are able to develop a sense of purpose as they begin to understand the business issues and what the company is trying to achieve.

Not only can employees tolerate honest disclosure, they are increasingly demanding it. At a recent speaking engagement for a national bank, I asked the program coordinator what issues she wanted me to address. "Just give us the facts," she said. "We want to hear the unadulterated truth, as you see it." I've come to believe that this is also what employees most want from their leaders. Certainly at the beginning of any large-scale transition, employees want straight answers to these tough questions:

- Will I keep my job?
- How will pay and benefits be affected?
- How will this affect my opportunities for advancement?
- Will I have a new boss?

- What new skills will I need?
- What will be expected of me?
- How will I be trained/supported for the new challenges?
- How will I be measured?
- What are the rewards or consequences?

Until these personal issues are resolved, employees are too preoccupied with their own situation to pay much attention to meeting the needs of the organization. It is advisable to take these sensitive issues head-on and volunteer to let people know where they stand. If leadership does not address these workplace concerns, the company rumor mill will speculate, gossip, embellish, trade half-truths and generally elevate the workforce's anxiety level.

When you can't answer every question, it is best to tell people that you understand their concern but don't know the answer. Or that you don't have the information yet, but will get back to them as soon as decisions are made. It is even better to tell people that you have the information but can't release it than to withhold or twist the truth. Not everyone will appreciate candid communication, but few will tolerate anything less.

During a major organizational restructuring, West Texas Utilities published the minutes of every meeting of the change-management task force to let all employees see how decisions were being evaluated and made. At first, the leadership at WTU thought so much candor might increase workforce resistance, but it soon became apparent that the more employees knew about the inner workings of the task force, the more readily they accepted the change proposed.

As the Chief Operating Officer at Adelphia, Ron Cooper and the rest of the executive team face a tough assignment: getting a company out of bankruptcy. Yet, even here, candid communication is a key strategy for engaging employees. According to Ron, "You've got to encourage an environment where people ask the hard questions and where management is responsive to those questions. Because when people feel they have information, it alleviates so much frustration. And that's true even if the answer to the question isn't positive. For example, in the situation we're in right now, there is still a lot of anxiety about what Adelphia needs to do to ultimately emerge from bankruptcy. Employees are concerned that one step in the process could result in significant layoffs. The fact of the matter is that we have no such layoffs planned. But if people have it on their mind, we would like them to ask that question so that we can tell them exactly how we're thinking about job security. Now I would never say to someone that there will be no layoffs in this company. But I will say that we aren't planning a massive reduction in force. And when we look at the numbers, which we share with employees, it's obvious that we have financial challenges in this business. But those challenges are on the revenue side, not on the cost side. When people understand how you've analyzed the problem, and how you relate that to the question they're asking about layoffs, and if you can convey that information in a way that's intelligible to them, then (hopefully) you can put that fear to rest."

Question #6: Can you answer the most important question: What's in it for them?

I was in Sweden working with a county government agency that was completely revamping its healthcare system. The leader of this enormous change was proud of the way he had communicated to the county's residents. They had been given a thorough briefing — the reasons behind the change, the timing of the change, and exactly how it was to be carried out. Then he turned to me with a frown, "But you know, there is still one question that I get asked all the time." I interrupted. "Let me guess," I said. "People want to know if the wait for a doctor's appointment will be any shorter than it currently is. Am I right?" The man looked startled.

"How did you know that?" he asked. I told him that I knew to expect that question because it is the one I hear most often about change — What's in it for me?

With Fluor Corporation's globally dispersed and project-focused workforce, past practice was that as projects came to an end, teams were reconfigured and re-mobilized to meet new requirements. Transfer of learning and experience was primarily limited to what employees brought directly to each new project assignment — and this was their power and how they were valued. When the company introduced an online knowledge-management tool, it also had to change these embedded workforce behaviors. One of the major factors that contributed to effecting that change was *Knowledge OnLine's* 24/7 pervasiveness and ease of con-nectability anywhere in the world. Employees quickly realized the benefits of sharing knowledge when they too could connect for their own benefit. This attitude took on an almost "grass roots" movement as the tool and methodologies caught on, and this atti-tude is a key factor in the cultural transformation and impact on work processes.

There are personal advantages to be found in almost every change, but people may need help discovering what the advan-tages are. Sometimes employees just need someone to guide them through a few questions: What are your career goals? What are the skills you would like to learn? What job-related experiences would you like have? In what ways might this change help you to fulfill some of your personal objectives? (It might be the chance to learn how to use new technology, the experience of serving on a change task force, an opportunity to make suggestions for improvements outside of your usual work area, a chance to be cross-trained in other needed skills, etc.)

Another way to point out possible advantages is by using real life examples of others who benefited during a similar change. If you implement an organization-wide change, but begin it in one department or division, you can use the success stories of people who have found personal advantages — learning and growth opportunities, increase in self-confidence, more job satisfaction — in the process.

Question #7: Is your communication "behavior-based?"

In San Francisco, on the corner of Powell and Market, street performers entertain tourists as they wait for the cable car to arrive. My favorite "act" is two fully dressed men who have spray-painted themselves gold and silver. Posing like statues, they kneel on the sidewalk facing each other with their elbows resting on a low platform and hands clasped in a traditional arm-wrestling position. In front of the man painted gold, there is a gold hat. In front of the silver man is a silver box. They stay absolutely motionless, until someone in the crowd puts a coin or a bill in one of the receptacles. If the money goes into the gold hat, the gilded man inches his arm forward gaining a slight advantage in the "wrestling match." They hold the new position and wait. If money goes into the silver box, then the silver man makes a move. All this is done in total silence. Neither man looks at nor speaks to the audience. They don't ask for money, and there is no sign instructing people about the procedure for or the result of making a contribution — yet the audience understands immediately what they are supposed to do. This is the essence of behavior-based communication.

Organizations send two concurrent sets of messages about change. One set of messages goes through formal channels of communications — speeches, newsletters, corporate videos, values statements and so forth. The other set of messages is "delivered" informally through a combination of "off the record" remarks and daily activities. When I coach senior management teams, I begin with two questions: 1) What do you currently do that already supports the change? and 2) What do you have to do differently to align with the change? For today's skeptical employee audience, rhetoric without action quickly disintegrates into empty slogans and company propaganda. Corporate leaders are beginning to learn the importance of behavior-based communication as a requirement for leading change. In the words of Sue Swenson, president of Leap Wireless, "What you do in the hallway is more powerful than anything you say in the meeting room."

Basically, behavior-based communications is a five-step process:

Step #1. Determine your current "values alignment." Create a "Say/Do" survey to find the gaps between what employees hear leadership say and what they see leadership do: Here is what our values state. What actions do you see us taking that are in alignment with our values? What behaviors are not in alignment?

Step #2. Communicate company *actions* to tell a common story to your stakeholders. Focus on business processes and practices that collectively define the corporation to employees, customers, shareholders and communities.

Step #3. Model the behaviors and attitudes you want from others. Gandhi said, "You must become the change you want to see in the world." If this is the classic "walk your talk" philosophy, I advise leaders to go even further and ask: What actions can you take right now to be used as examples in future communication? (What I refer to as the "walk *before* you talk" approach.) For example: If a company wanted to communicate its commitment to collaboration, I'd recommend holding off any corporate announcement until the senior management fully understood how their behavior had to change to be perceived as supportive of knowledge-sharing, until there was a system developed for teaching collaboration skills to employees and a process for educating managers as collaborative coaches, and until there was an appropriate shift from individual to team accomplishments in rewards and recognition programs.

Step #4. Create the corporate mechanisms that bring values into action. 3M allows scientists to spend 15 percent of their time working on whatever interests them, requires divisions to generate 30 percent of their revenues from new products introduced within the past four years, has an active internal venture capital fund, and grants prestigious awards for innovations. I don't know if 3M has a formal "values statement," but I know what they value.

Step #5. Track your progress. Alexian Brothers Hospitals have an executive with the title "Vice President of Mission Effectiveness," whose job is to make sure that the alignment between organizational values and actions remains intact.

Question #8: Can you paint the big-little picture?

Question: How do you eat an elephant?

Answer: One bite at a time.

A few years ago I was invited to speak at a function where top management was introducing a new corporate vision to initiate an organizational restructuring. It was quite an event. The goals of the organization had been written out in calligraphy on parchment paper and distributed to the 1,200 middle managers in the audience. The stage was decorated with an artistic backdrop — a shield with all the important corporate values symbolically displayed. I was the opening speaker. The chief executive officer followed me. Several other senior executives spoke, and then we all sat back and congratulated each other on a job well done.

At the luncheon that followed, a friend from the audience came up to me. "What did you think of the new corporate goals?" she asked. "Right on target," I responded enthusiastically. "And what about our values?" she continued. "Inspiring," I assured her. "I thought so too," she said. "Only one thing, though. We've been sitting in the audience all morning waiting for one of you to explain how we can possibly do all that."

We hadn't inspired that audience with the big picture — we'd overwhelmed them. It was a lesson I've never forgotten.

Vision is the big picture (we'll look at this next), and it is crucial to the success of the enterprise. But along with the big picture, people also need the little picture:

Big Picture: Presenting the concept of transformation.
Little Picture: How are we going to do that?
Big Picture: Setting long-term corporate goals.
Little Picture: Where do we begin?
Big Picture: Developing the overall objectives of the transformation.
Little Picture: What are the priorities?
Big Picture: Creating the mission of the organization.
Little Picture: Where does my contribution fit in?
Big Picture: Communicating organizational values.
Little Picture: What does this mean in my daily life?

Question #9: Is it your vision or our vision?

Leaders understand the power of vision to imbue people with a sense of purpose, direction and energy. A compelling vision of the future pulls people out of the seductive hold of the past and inspires them to set and reach ambitious corporate goals. Of even greater importance is the sense of meaning that people derive from their jobs when they can tie their contributions to the fulfillment of a clear, compelling vision. Leaders must therefore be able to paint the big picture. But if the vision belongs only to top management, it will never be an effective force for transformation. The power of a vision comes truly into play only when the employees themselves have had some part in its creation. So the crucial question becomes, "Whose vision is it?"

When the 20 top executives go away on a retreat to discuss the meaning of work and the future of the organization, they may return with a meaningful, well-crafted vision statement. But when they present this vision to their company, employees seldom find anything to connect with personally because they were never part of the discussion. If you want employees to feel the same kind of connection to their work that the executives felt at the retreat, then you have to get employees involved too. And when you involve people in creating a vision of the organization, their statements may reflect deep feelings. Chemical workers at DuPont in West Virginia created a statement that began: "We will make West Virginia, the United States, and the world a safer place."

So go off on a retreat to find your vision for the organization and the meaning in your work. Then talk about what you did and how you did it and invite everyone to make the vision come alive by discussing, aligning with, and owning it. Better yet — follow the lead of DuPont, and let people create their own vision. Here's an example of how a department might personalize a corporate vision:

1. Each department reviews the corporate vision as it was conceived by top leadership. (For example: A hospital's executives create a vision of "providing the best healthcare in the industry at the lowest cost." The executives communicate the vision throughout the hospital.)

2. Departments discuss how their specific functions support the overall vision and objectives. (The head of the hospital meets with the maintenance department to talk about the importance of cleanliness in reducing chances of infection and in aiding patient recovery. The department discusses the specific ways in which what they do affects the hospital's goals of patient care and cost containment.)

3. Departments create their own vision, which aligns with corporate vision. (The maintenance department creates its personal vision of "providing the best professional cleaning service in the most efficient manner.")

Question #10: Are you emotionally literate?

To be a consummate change agent, it is not enough to engage people's logic, you also have to appeal to their emotions. As leaders arrive at the insight that people skills (the "soft stuff" of business) hold the key to organizational change, human emotions take on new significance. Increasingly I am asked to consult with senior management to help them address the emotional turmoil that the workforce experiences around change. And it takes just a quick look at the recent past of corporate America to see how the workforce has been conditioned to respond so negatively. Look at it from the employees' point of view: The company is restructured, maybe merged with or taken over by another firm. All top management is replaced. There are massive layoffs, followed by rumors of more personnel cuts to come. No one knows the direction of the new organization or where to turn for guidance. Employees suffer "survivor guilt" and struggle under added workloads. People see dedicated co-workers being fired while on vacation, through messages left on answering machines, even in front of their children on "bring your daughter to work day." And from this emotionally damaged body, the work is still expected to flow as if nothing had happened and employees are automatically expected to embrace the next announced change.

Instead, negative emotional reactions spring from outrage and fear:

"First of all, you see the wrong people getting cut. You know some of these people; they have worked hard and done a good job for the company."

"They never even warned us. I had to read about the layoffs in the paper."

"The way they treated people was awful — with no concern for their feelings. At first I was relieved to be keeping my job, but then I started thinking that it could just as well have been me."

"I really felt sorry for my friends who were fired, but now I think they may have been the lucky ones."

Leaders who continue to think of change as a purely logical event will never understand the psychological pain it engenders in the workforce. I remember one research project I conducted for a regional president who had recently taken on his new position. "I am replacing a man who had been with the company for 20 years," he said. "I'm new to the organization and I'd like you to find out what employees need from me as their leader."

A week later I gave him my report. "I think you're going to like what I found," I began, "because what employees need most won't cost you anything. People aren't asking for additional pay or more support. What they are waiting for — and what they want from you more than anything else — is an acknowledgement of their distress." The employees in his division were waiting for someone to say to them: "You've lost a leader who was your friend, mentor and model. What a difficult time you must be having! I can only imagine how tough this is on you."

Large-scale organizational change almost invariably triggers the same sequence of emotional reactions — denial, negativity, a choice point, tentative acceptance, commitment. Leadership can either facilitate this emotional process — or ignore it at the peril of the transformation effort.

Denial

If the workforce has been *insufficiently prepared* for the reality of discontinuous change, people's initial reaction is usually shock and denial. People in shock are emotionally numb and refuse to believe that the change will take place. Informal conversations around the company begin with remarks like: "It will all blow over, it's just a matter of time," or "They'd never do that to us." At IBM in the 1980s, denial famously manifested in a "mainframe mindset" — the blind insistence that, in spite of the emergence of personal computers, big computers would reassert their market dominance. This reaction is not only to be anticipated in business enterprises, but can also occur in other populations. In one of my seminars for Chamber of Commerce executives, a participant reported that, in his city, people still spoke about the mining industry making a comeback. The mines had been closed for 20 years.

Because employees in denial refuse to believe the change will occur, there is little observable difference in their behaviors and attitudes, so it is easy for management to get the mistaken impression that people are having no difficulties handling the new situation. This is an inaccurate impression, of course — what appears to be acceptance of change is actually emotional numbness accompanying the shock of disbelief. If employee reaction to the announcement of a major change seems surprisingly passive, start asking questions!

In dealing with denial, leaders are faced with the challenge of making sure that all employees understand that the change is important, real and imminent. And the best way to ensure that is to involve people in the planning process from the very beginning. The earlier you gather employee input, encourage discussion and ask for ideas, the more it pays off in employee commitment and energy.

Negativity

When people have moved through the numbness of denial, they usually begin to have very negative feelings — self-doubt, fear, sadness, self-pity, depression, frustration, anger, grief and even hostility. At this point things seem to get worse. Typical responses you can expect include:

"I'm not going to put up with this without a fight."

"How could they do this to me after all I've done for them?"

"What will I do if I get laid off?"

"I'm powerless, so I might as well give up."

Whether combative or outwardly compliant, employees worrying about the personal impact of change or made resentful by the layoff of colleagues will have a hard time focusing on their jobs. During this phase of intense emotional reaction, managers can expect that absenteeism and mistakes will rise as productivity and morale decline.

Negativity is the most difficult emotional component for managers to deal with, but it's a natural part of the transformation process and must be faced. Leaders will find that it is counterproductive to ignore negative feelings, to punish employees for their "disloyal" attitude, or to attempt to "cheer up" people who are in obvious distress. What works best is to allow sufficient time for the reality of the proposed transformation to sink in, and then to schedule planning sessions to discuss employee concerns and feelings. By creating a safe place for people to express concern and criticism without judgement or fear of the consequences, you are helping them break through the negativity.

Resistance to change is normal. It should be anticipated and encouraged. Unexpressed negativity does not disappear, it goes underground to resurface later, often sabotaging an operation after the organization has made substantial investments in time, money and manpower. If management encourages a frank dialogue about fears and reservations early on, there is time to revamp systems to better support the change, intensify communication efforts, generate more employee involvement, develop strategic alternatives or (occasionally) even to jettison an unpopular plan. A forthright discussion also affords employees the opportunity to distinguish between those aspects of the change that might be able to be altered and those that are seen as central to the goals of the organization. If nothing else, encouraging people to express dissatisfaction lets them know that it is safe to disagree with management, that their concerns are being heard, and that their ideas and feelings are important. And by the way — if you can't facilitate this sort of process well yourself, it's a good idea to bring in someone who can.

The beginning of anything new always signals the death of the old. Changing the way work gets done means employees having to give up the competence and confidence they gained under the old system. Employees under new leadership must relinquish the relationships they created with their previous boss. A workforce relocating to new facilities has to leave behind the old building. With every "death" comes a period of mourning where people grieve for what they are being asked to leave behind. This is why you can expect that employees in the midst of a cultural transformation are almost certain to take a nostalgic look back at "the good old days" and to mourn the passing of that familiar culture.

Leaders of discontinuous change can focus on the future without describing the past as wrong. It is almost always unproductive to tell people that they must change to "correct" past performance. It is also unrealistic to speak of "correcting" in cases where the past has been highly successful. But in any case, it is wise to assume that workers have done their best in the past. Telling them it was not good enough — that, in effect, *they* were not good enough — is demoralizing, de-motivating, and guaranteed to build resentment.

Instead of blaming the old ways, leaders can help employees detach from the past by allowing them to mourn it. To facilitate people through the mourning period, the past must be honored in an almost ritualistic sense. From pictorial displays on company walls to parties celebrating the history of the organization, rituals help people say good-bye and move on.

Even employees going through an emotionally devastating situation, such as the closing of a plant, want to have the past honored. When, after more than a century of operation in the Lehigh Valley of Pennsylvania, Bethlehem Steel Corporation stopped making steel in its home city, the plant management team commissioned a video to commemorate the facility and pay tribute to the people who had worked there — in many cases for three and four generations of one family. The video was mailed to 2,900 active employees during the week the operations were closing. In a hostile labor-management environment, where 1,800 jobs were lost, only three people either refused to accept the video or returned it to management.

I don't mean to suggest that a commemorative video is the cure-all for employees' distress over losing jobs and closing facilities. But if those events are facts over which plant management has no control, then the question becomes how to deal with human beings facing the consequences of those facts. Leaders can either ignore people's suffering (the easier, less risky management choice) or confront it by paying tribute to the past. And, in fact, in the case of Bethlehem Steel, almost all employees were uniform in their praise for the video as a lasting memento and for its sensitivity to the subject and the people.

Rituals can play a powerful part in any organizational transformation. The internal merger of the communications and information systems divisions of a telecommunications company was described by Mitchell Marks, in his book, *Charging Back Up the Hill.* A ceremony was created to help people bury the past and prepare for the future. Managers from both groups were brought together and asked to write down the three worst things that could happen to them as a result of the merger. Each one also received a sheet of his preintegration letterhead and an old business card. Managers were then led outside and assembled around a wooden casket. As

a band played a funeral march, people crumpled up their statements, cards, and letterheads and tossed them into the coffin. When
they were finished, a 100-ton paver came rolling around the corner.
As it approached the coffin, the band burst into the spirited tune
"On Wisconsin" and the group cheered as the paver rolled over
the coffin, flattening it and its contents. As soon as this was over,
the group was taken back inside, given caps and gowns to wear,
and assembled in an auditorium where a banner proclaimed,
"Congratulations, Graduates!" The regional president gave a graduation speech that ended with the words: "It is now your turn: our
destiny lies in your generation's hands!" Then the "graduates"
were marched on stage, given a diploma ("master of merger management") and a graduation gift — a share of company stock.

The Choice Point

The choice point is a period of vacillating emotions as people in
the workforce choose whether or not to support the transformation. There is a schism in organizations going through transition,
as the more change-adept employees move into new roles and relationships while others stand firm in their opposition — which
leaves the undecided majority feeling much like the taffy in a taffy
pull. The schizophrenia of going through a transition is expressed
by people's comments:

"Maybe this will be for the best, but on the other hand ..."

"I'm not sure that I can meet the new challenges, but
perhaps..."

Leaders help employees through transition by giving them
honest information about requirements for future success within
the organization. It is important to discover and tell the stories of
company "heroes" — those workers whose behaviors exemplify
success under the new model. (If you are transforming the organization to be more customer-responsive, then have customers rate

your service on a scale of 1 to 10, and make an example of the first team of employees who receive a score of 8 or higher.) The benefits of communicating employee success stories are twofold: First, it is an opportunity to recognize and reward the change-adept who have already embraced transformation. Second, it provides all employees with real-life examples of theory moving into practice by showing what it takes to be successful.

Better yet, let the employees tell their own stories. When the two UK insurance giants Royal and SunAlliance merged, the communications department launched a radio program on cassette and CD aimed at people who wanted to make change happen, but were not sure how. The program included "real people" telling their stories in their own words. This proved to be very powerful in communicating change.

It is also important for each individual to assess his or her skills in light of the current job market. Those who have been with the company for a long time are probably unaware of what is available to them in the wider employment world. A thorough assessment of their skills and aptitudes can prepare employees for making good choices within the new structure.

As people consider letting go of the past, they will be looking for something to replace their losses. The leader's role is to create *linkage* between the transformed corporation and its employees. The concept of linkage goes beyond making sure that everyone knows where the company is headed, what's expected of them and how their contributions fit into the overall strategy — although all of those concepts are vitally important. True linkage — the kind that bonds committed employees to the success of the organization — comes when there is alignment between the values of the company and those of the workforce. As a leader, the most effective way of developing this powerful linkage is to encourage employees to clarify their own personal goals and values and to see how they fit within the vision of the transformed organization.

Linkage Exercise

Step #1 — **Define your personal values.**

How do you define success in life?

How do you want to be remembered?

Step #2 — **Decide what your professional "purpose" is.**

What do you want to accomplish in your career?

Why?

What are you passionate about achieving?

Step #3 — **Write out your goals.**

What are your professional goals for this year?

What are your professional goals for the next five years?

Step #4 — **Describe your ideal working environment.**

Under what working conditions are you the happiest and most productive?

Step #5 — **Write out the values and principles of the organization.**

What attitudes and behaviors does the company value?

What organizational principles would you be fired for violating?

Step #6 — **Link your goals and values to the organization.**

How do the values of the organization reflect your own values?

How do the changes going on within the company afford you new opportunities to reach your goals?

There is no single organizational culture and no universal set of corporate values that is right for every worker. I've interviewed employees in paternalistic companies who were uncomfortable with paternalism: "I wish they'd stop calling this a family. It isn't. It's a business. But that doesn't mean we still can't treat each other with caring and respect." I've talked with highly paid workers in *Fortune* 500 organizations who felt lost in an anonymous sea of faces: "I'd love to work for a small company where I knew my contribution really mattered." And I've heard the opposite lament from employees working in home offices for entrepreneurial startups: "I really miss the interaction of meeting face-to-face with members of a team. I wish I were with a big, bustling enterprise." The idea is not to try to become all things for all employees, but rather to have your culture so well defined and promoted that employees looking for a values-match know exactly what they are getting.

One of the most emotionally distressing situations is created when people try to thrive in a business environment that doesn't support their personal principles or goals. And if that alignment is seriously askew, the best thing for both the organization and the employee would be to help the worker find a new job in a different organization. But the need to sever the current business relationship is less frequent than you might expect. The purpose of a linkage exercise is to help employees make connections between their goals and beliefs and the opportunities that the organization offers. An unexpected research result of using this exercise in hundreds of companies was the discovery that regardless of the outcome, the very process of clarifying personal values and goals caused employees to be more supportive of their organizations.

Acceptance

Once people have agreed to support the change, they are ready for action. Organizations in the early stages of the acceptance phase are characterized by abrupt increases of energy and enthusiasm. Informal conversations will begin with: "I've got another idea," "Where do you suppose this might fit in?" and "How do we get started?" The management challenge at this point is to focus and channel this energy by restating the overall vision, giving employees access to all information needed to understand the dynamics of the transformation, and to emphasize the need to collaborate with others and to experiment with various solutions. It may feel as though you are starting over from the beginning — and indeed, in some respects you are. But remember that workers in emotional turmoil probably didn't absorb much until now. So, back to the basics: Where is the organization heading? Why is the organization changing? What will the work priorities be for your team? What are the organization's new core competencies? What are the new job skills and accountabilities?

The potential for innovative and creative ideas will never be higher than now, when the old structure is crumbling and the new only exists in the realm of imagination. To focus creative energy in this chaotic environment, leaders should:

- Offer training in creativity and innovative problem-solving.
- Urge workers to question every existing workplace rule and regulation.
- Plan events — picnics, after-hours get-togethers, pizza parties — to unify the previously fragmented organization.
- Encourage a workplace atmosphere filled with the fun and joy of creating something new.
- Set short-term goals with immediate payoffs.
- Initiate pilot projects to encourage experimentation.

Commitment

Commitment is the final phase of the change process; it is where workers emotionally invest themselves in the new organization. When employees are committed to the success of the transformation, it is again reflected in their questions:

"Why didn't we do this five years ago?"

"What are we going to do next?"

Commitment is a time for celebration. To have transformed an enterprise *and* engaged the enthusiasm of the workforce is a tribute to leadership and employees. This fact needs to be acknowledged and celebrated throughout the organization.

Commitment is also a time for rewards. Demonstrate the results the organization has achieved by bringing in customers, suppliers, and competitors to talk about benefits from their perspectives. Single out those individuals and teams whose achievements were outstanding — but find ways to thank everybody for their contribution.

Above all, commitment is a time for learning. Leaders who utilize a Living-Systems Model of change help employees realize that: 1) discontinuous change is a never-ending, life-enhancing process of leaps to new forms, and 2) adaptive behaviors can be learned and incorporated into more effective strategies for the future. The commitment phase offers a unique opportunity for the entire workforce to think back through the change and find the strategies, behaviors and attitudes that were the most effective with this transition to prepare for the next one.

Post-Change Questionnaire

Employees
- How did you feel initially about the change?
- What helped you get through any negative feelings?
- To whom did you turn for support?
- What did leaders do exceptionally well?
- What do leaders need to improve for next time?
- What personal strategies, attitudes and work practices served you best?
- What was the final outcome and how did you influence that outcome?
- What did you learn about yourself?
- What do you plan to do differently next time?

Leaders
- How did you feel initially about the change?
- How did you handle any negative feeling of your own when dealing with employees?
- To whom did you turn for support?
- What management strategies served you best?
- What did you learn about your leadership skills?
- What did you learn about yourself?
- What did you learn about your employees?
- What do you plan to do differently next time?

Question #11: Do you know what shouldn't change?

The greatest challenge for leaders is to know the difference between what has to be preserved and what needs to be changed. The "genius" of leadership is being able to preserve an organization's core values, and yet change and adapt as times require. And the product of that kind of leadership is an organization that goes on for a very long time.

Robert Burnside, the Chief Learning Officer of Ketchum, gave me a practical example of the kind of discussion that needs to take place around this issue: "Let's look at 1999 versus 2003. Do our values change when the marketplace changes so dramatically? The answer is absolutely not. Values are eternal. However, what we do need to change is our behaviors in relation to the changed marketplace. That's the discussion our senior management is currently having. We're looking at how to encourage changes in behavior that are still in alignment with our values."

Question #12: Are you telling the right stories?

I'm often introduced as a change-management expert married to a man who refuses to change anything. So, during my speeches, I tell humorous stories about the resistance that Ray puts up —

and how I learned, from managers I'd interviewed, different ways to handle his protests.

After every speech, audience members come up to me to comment on my husband. Many people recognize their co-workers or loved ones (or themselves!) in him, and some jokingly commiserate with me. The thing I find most intriguing about this phenomenon is that in my 20 years of professional speaking, no one has ever approached me after a program to say they most appreciated my "fifth point." That's because they don't remember what my fifth point was. But they *do* remember Ray and the lessons about handling change resistance that they learned through my stories.

And herein lies a lesson for leaders. Social scientists note that there are two different modes of cognition: the paradigmatic mode and the narrative mode. The former is rooted in rational analysis; the latter is represented in fairy tales, myth, legends, metaphors, anecdotes and stories. Good stories are more powerful than plain facts!

This is not to reject the value in facts, of course, but simply to recognize their limits in influencing people. People "hear" a story much better than they hear facts. Stories supplement analysis. Facts are neutral. People make decisions based on what facts *mean* to them, not on the facts themselves. Facts aren't influential until they mean something to someone. Stories give facts meaning.

Here is another difference: Trying to influence people through scientific analysis is a "push" strategy. It requires the speaker to convince the listener through cold, factual evidence. Storytelling is a "pull" strategy, in which the listener is invited to join the experience as a participant and to imagine acting on the mental stage the storyteller creates. Stories resonate with adults in ways that can bring them back to a childlike open-mindedness — and make them less resistant to experimentation and change. Facts remind them of school!

Compared to facts, stories are better for building community, capturing the imagination, and exerting influence. Stories about the past help employees understand the rich heritage of an organization, stories about early adopters offer successful examples of dealing with change, personal stories are powerful leadership tools for building trust, humorous stories can ease tension and, if you interview key staff, stories can capture their wisdom.

Question #13: Are you having fun?

Washington Mutual Bank linked entertainment with change-management when it launched an internal branding campaign. The idea was to create events that communicated Washington Mutual's brand promise and brand attributes in a way that was fun, informal and, most importantly, memorable. The events typically lasted between 60–90 minutes. Staff would arrive at the venue to be met by "cheerleaders and greeters." The events were designed to be a celebration of the brand, so the mood was kept festive and light-hearted. An especially created brand jingle was played and employees were invited to participate in "brand games" to win prizes. External consultants — known as "infotainers" — regaled the audience with amusing songs and sketches focusing on the brand attributes and associated behavior. The CEO — or local managers in the case of smaller events — spoke about the brand initiative for about 20–25 minutes. A video was shown to reinforce the message and the infotainers wrapped up events with more entertainment designed to drive home the key brand messages. Managers were intentionally involved in games and antics in an effort to humanize the campaign and use company role models to reinforce key messages in a fun way.

But even change that isn't so positive can be helped by a spirit of humor and fun. Vanessa Wittman was hired as the chief financial officer at 360networks a few months before the initial public offering (IPO): "In the 14 months that followed, we took the company public, raised a few billion dollars, bought several companies, and filed for bankruptcy. Then we spent 17 months in bankruptcy. I had the same team through this whole wild ride, and I didn't lose any of my core folks. But I did need to redirect my team's commitment from 'let's go make this company the Global Crossing killer' to 'let's get this company out of bankruptcy.' The biggest motivator I used was acknowledging the pain of what was happening to all of us, then making sure they saw the current challenge and the benefit of meeting that challenge. I had an incredible group of people who really bonded over trying to get the company out. We used to sit in meetings late at night preparing for bank sessions, thinking, 'This is just painfully horrible. Why are we having so much fun?' If you can go after big, complex goals with a real sense of purpose, while maintaining your sense of humor, even the tough stuff becomes interesting, motivating — and even fun!"

When you have answered all these questions to your own satisfaction, you will have taken a giant step on the road to transforming yourself into a first-rate change agent.

CHAPTER 5

THE CORE OF LEADERSHIP

"How can I take control if you keep holding on?"

"Leadership is not about job title. It isn't even a matter of style. At the core, it comes down to two simple questions: What kind of person are you? And are those personal qualities inspiring to others?"

**E. David Coolidge III,
Vice Chairman and CEO,
William Blair & Company**

LEADERSHIP IS THE ART of engaging the hearts and minds of ordinary people to achieve extraordinary results, I tell my audiences.

"But how do *you* know what it takes to lead an organization?" the audiences ask back.

Good question. And the answer is, I *don't* know. At least not from personal experience. But neither do the multitude of psychologists, sociologists and historians who have written volumes on the theoretical nature of leadership. Because, in the end, the only people who really know how it works are the leaders themselves. This chapter is devoted to 14 of those leaders. Fourteen highly successful men and women who have dealt with challenges of change throughout their careers. They all confronted the new business age head on, saw what needed to be done and said, "Let's get going!"

Robert Burnside, Chief Learning Officer, Ketchum

Robert Burnside is the chief learning officer at Ketchum, a top-10 global public relations firm and unit of Omnicom. Burnside is responsible for the agency's professional development program, which includes leadership development, core business skills and practice- and industry-specific expertise. The program is housed under Ketchum College, an institution long recognized for its focus on bringing learning and development opportunities to Ketchum colleagues around the globe. Prior to joining Ketchum, Burnside was vice president of operations for Corporate University Xchange. He also worked for 14 years with the Center for Creative Leadership, rated the number one executive leadership institution by *BusinessWeek*.

Joan M. Crockett, Senior Vice President, Human Resources, Allstate Insurance Company

Joan Crockett is responsible for developing the full range of policies and programs designed to attract, retain and reward Allstate employees and agents. Her specific responsibilities include recruiting/selection, job and organizational design, compensation and benefits, leadership development, education and development, performance management, employee relations and workforce diversity. Additionally, she serves as a member of the Allstate senior management team. In 1997, Crockett was named Human Resource Executive of the Year by *Human Resource Executive* magazine.

E. David Coolidge III, Vice Chairman and Chief Executive Officer, William Blair & Company

Dave Coolidge joined William Blair 35 years ago. Coolidge, who was manager of the firm's Corporate Finance department from 1977–1994, currently is a director of the Securities Industry Association. He is a trustee of both Williams College and the University of Chicago, and plays an active role in several other organizations. He is a trustee of Rush-Presbyterian-St Luke's Medical Center, a director at the Better Government Association and Youth Guidance, an advisory board member at Northwestern University's Kellogg Graduate School of Management, a member of the Civic Committee of the Commercial Club of Chicago, and a board member of Kmart Holding Corporation.

Robert L. Dilenschneider, President and Chief Executive Officer, The Dilenschneider Group

Prior to forming his own public relations firm, Bob Dilenschneider served from 1986 to 1991 as president and CEO of Hill and Knowlton, Inc., where he tripled that firm's revenues to nearly $200 million and delivered more than $30 million in profit. Dilenschneider has counseled major corporations, professional groups, trade associations and educational institutions, and has assisted clients in dealings with regulatory agencies, labor unions, consumer groups and minorities, among others. He has authored eight books — including the best-selling *Power and Influence.* Most recently, he published *50 Plus! — Critical Career Decisions for the Rest of Your Life.*

Gloria Feldt, President, Planned Parenthood Federation

Gloria Feldt is president of Planned Parenthood Federation of America. Planned Parenthood is the nation's largest and most trusted voluntary reproductive health care organization serving nearly five million women, men and teens every year. PPFA-I programs work in more than 20 countries. Feldt has led the organization through a major revitalization, resulting in the adoption of the Planned Parenthood Vision for 2025. She has received a number of honors, including recognition as one of *Vanity Fair's* Top 200

Women Leaders, Legends, and Trailblazers of 1998 and one of *Glamour* magazine's 2003 Women of the Year. A frequent public speaker and media commentator, she is the author of *Behind Every Choice Is a Story.*

Jean M. Halloran, Senior Vice President, Human Resources, Agilent Technologies

As senior vice president of Human Resources, Jean Halloran's responsibilities include directing Agilent's global policies and programs for leadership and talent development, compensation, benefits, staffing and workforce planning, human resources systems, education and organization development. Halloran has wide experience in human resources, extending back to when she joined Hewlett-Packard Company's Medical Products Group in 1980. Halloran has also been a director of several schools and non-profit organizations, including Concord Academy, the Human Resources Policy Institute, and Jobs for the Future.

Christie Hefner, Chairman and Chief Executive Officer, Playboy Enterprises

As chairman and chief executive of Playboy Enterprises Inc. and chairman of Playboy.com Inc., Christie Hefner oversees policy, management and strategy in all areas of Playboy Enterprises. During her tenure, she has restructured operations, eliminated unprofitable businesses and initiated successful international expansion in publishing, entertainment and new media, and in 1994, she led the company onto the Internet, when Playboy became the first national magazine on the World Wide Web.

Joseph P. Pieroni, President, Sankyo Pharma Inc.

As president of the U.S. subsidiary of Sankyo Co., Ltd. — one of the world's leading pharmaceutical companies and discoverer of the statin class of lipid-lowering drugs — Joe Pieroni brings 30 years of global pharmaceutical expertise to the leadership of Sankyo's U.S. operations. He was responsible for assembling the leadership team that established Sankyo's strong sales and marketing presence in the United States in 1996. Pieroni's background in chemistry and business combine with his recognized leadership skill to create a unique organization whose entrepreneurial spirit draws on the best qualities of each team member to grow a successful organization.

Lura J. Powell, Ph.D., President, Lura J. Powell & Associates and Senior Associate, Washington Advisory Group

Before starting her own consulting firm in 2003, Lura Powell was a senior vice president and officer of Battelle and director of the Pacific Northwest National Laboratory, operated by Battelle for the U.S. Department of Energy. As director, Powell ensured that PNNL delivered breakthroughs in the fields of fundamental science, environmental science and technology, energy and national security, and rapidly translated them into commercial practice. She also led the Laboratory as it prepared to play a major role in systems biology. Powell's leadership of PNNL earned her the Department of Energy's Distinguished Associate Award, and the National Nuclear Security Administration's Distinguished Service Gold Medal.

Horst Schulze, former President and Chief Operating Officer, The Ritz-Carlton Hotel Company

A man of rare ability and vision, Horst Schulze created a new world of elegance, service and beauty while he served as the founding president and chief operating officer of The Ritz-Carlton Hotel Company. Under Schulze's direction, The Ritz-Carlton Hotels won an unprecedented two Malcolm Baldrige National Quality Awards in the service category.

Frederick W. Smith, Chairman, President and Chief Executive Officer, Federal Express Corporation

Fred Smith founded Federal Express in 1971. Best known for setting industry standards with its innovative use of technology and service excellence, the company has approximately 119,000 employees in 210 countries throughout the world. In 1990, FedEx became the first company to win the Malcolm Baldridge National Quality Award in the service category, and in 1994 became the first global express transportation company to receive simultaneous worldwide ISO 9001 certification.

Sue Swenson, President and Chief Operating Officer, Leap Wireless

Recognized throughout the wireless industry for her strong operational background, Sue Swenson brings more than 22 years of telecommunications industry expertise to leading Leap's overall operations. Prior to joining Leap in July 1999, she served as president and CEO of Cellular One (now AT&T Wireless), the joint venture between Vodafone AirTouch and AT&T Wireless in San Francisco, for five years. Prior to joining Cellular One, Swenson held executive operating positions at Pacific Bell and PacTel Cellular. Leap, headquartered in San Diego, California, provides innovative communications solutions for the mass consumer market.

Steven Wikstrom, Co-Chief Executive Officer, Reell Precision Manufacturing Corporation

Steve Wikstrom is the co-CEO of Reell Precision Manufacturing Corporation, a $35 million company that produces wrap spring clutches and constant torque hinges for foreign and domestic customers. Reell has been the subject of several news articles outlining its innovative business practices and ethical conduct. It's one thing to talk about spirituality and integrity for your organization; it's another thing to live them day to day. Reell (German for integrity)

Precision Manufacturing has been widely recognized as a company that has striven to integrate the two for over three decades.

Vanessa Wittman, Executive Vice President and Chief Financial Officer, Adelphia Communications

Vanessa Wittman is the executive vice president and chief financial officer of Adelphia Communications Corporation, the fifth-largest cable television company in the country. She was named to Adelphia's management team in March 2003. Prior to Adelphia, Wittman was chief financial officer of broadband network services provider 360networks, where she led the company's restructuring efforts and successful emergence from bankruptcy protection in November 2002.

I've selected these leaders to represent the widest possible range of experience. Each of the 14 has his or her unique corporate responsibilities to carry out. Each represents an organization that is affected in specific ways by the new global economy, the IT revolution, the disappearance of stable currency values worldwide and the collapse of the old Industrial structure as an organizing model for their companies. But all share one thing in common: an apparently innate set of emotional and intellectual qualities that make up what I call the Core of Leadership. The components of that core are: 1) vision, 2) integrity, 3) trust, 4) values, 5) vulnerability, and 6) motivation. Together they produce what we all instantly recognize as leaders. But we aren't just talking about special skills or strategies these people exercise, we're talking about individual character. Like the force of gravity or the lump of uranium in a nuclear generator, the leadership core works invisibly. And like any living system, it sometimes works intuitively and mysteriously. But its positive effects upon others can be readily observed, and those observations, in turn, can be put to immediate use by anyone charged with leading fellow employees at any level of an organization.

LEADERSHIP AS VISION

In contrast to control-minded authority of the past, today's leaders must exercise power through a shared purpose and vision. An organizational vision is not the same as long-range or even strategic planning. Planning is a linear process, progression toward a goal. Vision is more holistic — a sense of direction that combines a good business strategy with a comprehensive organizational purpose that declares its own importance. A vision describes a business as it *could* become over the long term and outlines a feasible way of achieving this goal. People look to leaders for direction. To transform an organization, leaders must adopt and communicate a vision of the future that impels people beyond the boundaries and limits of the past.

Leaders have a visionary mindset. They *create* a mental picture of the change they want to manifest. Leaders have the vision to forecast what's next and the passion to reach into the future and seek out new opportunities to push for greater outcomes. It is incredibly important that leaders clearly articulate the vision, and set expectations through the images they create and the stories they tell.

Leaders who articulate such visions aren't mystics, but broad-based thinkers who are willing to take risks. Visionary leaders don't have to be brilliant, highly innovative, or incredibly charismatic. But they do have to be intently focused on what it is they are trying to achieve. Fred Smith of FedEx put it in these very practical terms: "If there is *any* indication that the leader is not totally committed to achieving the vision, then all the sweet talk in the world will not get people to support it."

Burnside: Let's say that I tell my direct reports: "Our goal next year is $200 million." Well, that's a goal — maybe even a stretch goal — and it's clear. And I can have a long conversation with my team about the kinds of investments we're going to make to get there, who we have to hire, whether we're considering some merger and acquisition activity, and so forth. But I haven't yet tapped into a reason *why* the goal is of value. For that, people need a vision that aligns with their personal sense of what's right and good to do in the world. Vision essentially implies that there is an image of the future that we can all hold in our imaginations that is motivational for us. So the vision adds motivation to the goal.

Crockett: A good leader has to be a storyteller. Storytelling enables the leader to connect with employees on an emotional level. The leader needs to paint a picture of where we're going, and it has to be a picture that is not only clear but also exciting, compelling and inclusive. People have to see where they fit into the vision. Executing a vision is never a linear process. You're always going to have your share of frustrations, setbacks and disappointments. The leader often has to re-energize and reinvent the story and make it continually exciting.

Everyone, at some time, takes up the role of leader/storyteller. At some point, each individual in the organization tells the story of the vision to others. They talk about what they do and where their company is going. They discuss it at home with their families, and at parties with their friends. Employees who are energized about and have pride in their company will tell the story from their own perspectives — in their own words, in their own way. And their vision will line up very neatly with the story the leader has just told.

Feldt: Leadership is about creating meaning for an organization — and nothing creates meaning better than having a vision of where we want to go and what we want to accomplish. I'm basically the leader of a social movement, and most people in this movement don't report to me. So the way we set our vision for the future was to engage everyone in that conversation. The resulting document is called "The Planned Parenthood Vision for 2025." We started this process in 2000 and chose to look 25 years ahead so that people could distance themselves from whatever they were afraid of losing in what they are doing today. That freed people to think in a much more expansive way than they would have if we'd been crafting a strategic plan for the next three years.

We started out by commissioning a research project. Consultants interviewed experts in all of the different fields that we have an interest in — everything from reproductive healthcare to gender and population issues to politics. And we used this research to provide background information for everybody throughout the organization who requested it. In this way, most people were prepared by the time we held our first meeting for key national office staff, volunteers, affiliate CEOs and board chairs.

We trained "vision facilitators" to guide the conversation for the national organization, at each and every affiliate, and among the different constituents — medical directors, clinic directors, educators, etc. Although my views were strongly represented, everyone's input was considered, and we formally ratified the vision at our annual conference. The entire process took about 18 months. A long time? Sure. But the result is a powerful vision for the future that is *owned* by all of us.

Halloran: Leadership as vision is partly foresight, knowing where you are trying to take the business, and partly the communication skill to describe that future so people can see themselves as part of it. But it's also the process of inviting people to help create the vision, and then listening — sincerely listening — so that people really feel included. It's amazing how much people are willing to give of themselves if you ask for help. And there is something inherently creative and motivating about painting a vision together as opposed to just receiving one that's told to you.

Pieroni: This is one of the most important aspects of leadership. I've seen what happens when an organization has no vision. In one company I worked for, lack of vision created a tremendous amount of confusion and dissatisfaction. So I strongly believe in creating a vision — a perception of what things *could be*. As a leader, you really put yourself out on a limb because you are really talking about future possibilities — many of which may not material-ize. And people need to know that up front. Still, a "stretch vision" should be just that — a picture of what is possible.

Here's how it works in practical application: In pharmaceuti-cal research, we need a long-term vision because products we're working on today won't materialize for at least 10 years. So we have a strategic management group that meets once a year to cre-ate a strategic plan and work on the vision — how the company will look in the next five years and in the five years after that. Once this group is in agreement, we present this vision to the rest of the organization (multiple times) so that everyone sees the same pic-ture of where we are now, where we are headed in the mid-term, and where we think we could be 10 years from now.

Powell: If you want an organization to move forward, to be successful in the long term, a leader really needs to have a vision for the future and the ability to get others to own that vision. When I first came to Pacific Northwest National Laboratory, I learned that, although the Laboratory had a long history of biological research, it had missed out on the genome revolution. I wanted to make sure we didn't miss out on the post-genome revolution, which will bring the knowledge derived from the genomes of humans, microbes, plants and animals to solve real-world prob-lems. So I focused on establishing a strong program in systems biology that would position the Lab as a key leader with key skills in post-genomic science that would be important for our customers, the Department of Energy and other funding agencies. I knew from past experience that integrating biotechnology broadly into a pre-dominately physical sciences and engineering organization could create resistance. Yet I saw the integration of the biological sciences with the physical sciences and the information sciences as the major wave of the future. But that was *my* vision. Rather than "ordering" people to accept it, we embarked together on a planning session that included the top scientists and engineers as well as other leaders throughout the organization. Ultimately, although it took some time, management and staff not only understood the importance of building a strong systems biology program, but backed the idea of putting major resources into building this program, because they could see how it was going to ultimately enhance the future of their own programs. In the end, people have to feel that the vision belongs to them.

Swenson: Vision makes a huge impact on an organization. And it is even more important when conditions are changing than when things are relatively static. Leaders need to create a compelling vision about where the organization is going, gain commitment to it, and bring that vision into reality by making the necessary organizational changes. To do this, leaders need to manage the business strategically and give employees the confidence that they can lead the organization to that vision.

Wittman: By nature I'm practical and pragmatic — and a bit of a cynic. So for somebody like me, a long-term vision without tangible steps isn't motivating. Bill Schleyer, the chairman and CEO of Adelphia, has an amazing ability to understand both the elevated vision and the "roll up your sleeves" details. It still stuns me to hear Bill talk about the "post-emergence" company we have a chance to become at Adelphia and then, five minutes later, to watch him grinding through what has to get done in the next 10 days to keep us on track. I'm not particularly inspired by someone who stays at the "50,000-foot level," but I am deeply impressed by Schleyer's ability to understand and own both the future vision and today's hard, granular facts.

An exercise I use with leaders to help them clarify their personal vision begins with imagining themselves five years in the future. Utilizing full-sensory imagery techniques (where they realistically imagine that they, the organization, and the world are five years further on), I ask them to respond to the following questions:

Vision Exercise

- **When you look around your company, what do you see happening? What do you hear? What do you feel?**
  A woman who had recently left the major consulting firm she had worked at for 12 years and started her own company with two clients, three employees, and small offices in an old building in Oakland, California, responded this way:
  "As I walk into the lobby of our new offices in San Francisco, the first thing I'm aware of is the energy level. We are so busy — staff is meeting with clients, working on computers, talking on telephones, gathering in small groups to compare war stories and share successes. We have at least 30 new employees here and it is a truly diverse mix of people — ages, ethnic backgrounds, married, singles — and I see a variety of clothing styles from business suits to blue jeans. I'm proud to see the kind of entrepreneurship we have created in the organization. Employees behave as if they own the business. We are very successful and highly profitable."

- **What kind of culture does the organization have?**
  "It is a collaboration of professionals. There is a unity of purpose supported by full communication of basic business information. The culture is open, relaxed and vibrant."

- **What kinds of products or services do you now offer?**
  "We have expanded beyond consulting services to include a highly successful series of leadership training programs for corporate managers. And we've opened offices in Chicago and New York."

- **What is it like to be one of your employees?**
  "Employees love working here. People know their expertise is

valued because they can see the direct link between their efforts, corporate profits and their bonus pay. They feel respected because they're given the freedom to make critical business decisions, and they are energized and excited by the challenges of the future — to be the best change-management consulting firm in the business. They also enjoy working here because we have a philosophy that includes laughter, play and fun. We support each other and have a good time together."

- **What is it like to be a customer?**
  "Customers are constantly delighted by our firm's professionalism, friendliness and flexibility. They especially appreciate our ability to utilize their own employees in creating and delivering our services, so that success is shared right from the beginning of a project."

- **What is it like to be a competitor?**
  "Our competitors are occasionally our clients, our collaborators, and our resources — so we engage in a friendly rivalry that spurs higher levels of performance in all of us."

- **What is it like to be a stockholder?**
  "We are a privately held company."

- **What effect is your company having on the community? On society? On the environment?**
  "Our company has adopted a community project — a battered-women's shelter — which we support with money and personal time. We also feel that our work benefits society in general because our consulting services result in businesses becoming more profitable while creating a work environment that is more personally fulfilling for employees."

- **What effect has your leadership had on the people in your firm?**
  "I have helped talented people discover their strengths, build their abilities, and use those strengths and abilities."

Doing this exercise, I always have participants close their eyes and see the future — rather than simply discussing future objectives. I know when this has been accomplished because people begin to describe their visions in very personal and emotional terms — at which point I tell them that holding onto this personal, emotional quality is what makes the vision come alive when they communicate it to others.

Remember, though, sharing your personal vision is only the beginning. Unless you engage the workforce in the process of crafting the vision, they won't truly own it. When Dick Kleine was the general manager of the Harvester Works at John Deere, the company adopted lean manufacturing principles — and totally transformed the way combines were made. "We started with a group of 14 employees — about half out of the shop and half from the office — and got them together to write a vision statement about the way we want to be. They came up with 10 parts to that aspiration — including communication, trust, job satisfaction, and customer satisfaction. That document became the vision that drove employees toward change."

Leadership as Integrity

A corporate task force at Federal Express identified integrity as a key leadership component necessary for successful leaders within FedEx. They defined integrity this way: Adheres firmly to a code of business ethics and moral values; behaves consistently with corporate values and professional responsibility; does not abuse management privileges; gains and maintains trust/respect; serves as a consistent role model in support of corporate policies, professional ethics, and corporate culture; does what is morally and ethically right.

Integrity goes beyond merely being honest. Although it certainly includes honesty. It is about the match between what leaders say and what they do. According to the executives in my sample, leading with integrity also implies a willingness to embody the attitudes and behaviors you want to see in employees.

Dilenschneider: If a leader doesn't have integrity, he or she might not be found out right away, but they will eventually. And, at that point, everything they might have accomplished will go into ruin. So a leader *has* to have integrity. And, by the way, integrity is a lot more than honesty. It also involves respect and trust and treating people well. People who I think have enormous integrity include Ed Breen, who took over from Dennis Kozlowski as chief executive officer of Tyco International. Ed has integrity a mile long and a mile deep, and he has fixed his integrity to this company which has had serious problems. Another person with high integrity is Marilyn Carlson Nelson. Marilyn runs a $35 billion enterprise — the biggest travel company in the world. She tends to draw a circle in which people are invited in to trust one another and reach for the same goals. Through the force of her personal integrity, over the years she has built an organization of over 100,000 employees who believe in the same things and do things correctly.

Crockett: There is nothing more important in the insurance industry than integrity. In our business, we sell a promise. That's what we say to customers every day: "You are paying for our promise to fill your needs when the time comes." And if we don't deliver what we promise, we'll be out of business. It's just that simple.

It's one thing when our chairman states that we'll stand by our word, but it's with each of our agencies and each of our claims employees who actually face the customer that the promise gets tested. There are occasions in everybody's job, every day, where integrity comes into play. Leaders need to stay vigilant, to reinforce integrity, and ensure that their actions send the right signals to employees.

The equity in your corporate reputation can be wiped out in an instant — it only takes one inappropriate decision. Integrity is one of Allstate's core values — it's a filter used in every decision-making process. If a decision feels like a bad fit with your value system, it is most likely the wrong move even if it means sacrificing some short-term gain.

Halloran: Integrity basically boils down to two things: Do I make commitments that I intend to keep, and do I do what I say I'm going to? So, at the front end — am I willing to make commitments and let people know "this is who I am and what I can add," but not make more of a commitment than I can reasonably deliver? And then, once I have committed, can I be counted on to fulfill my commitment? That to me is the heart of integrity.

Wikstrom: We need employees to be responsible — which to us means trustworthy and accountable. In our company we try to create relationships that allow us to "call" one another on behavior that doesn't meet this standard. A recent example occurred during the development of our latest strategic plan. Every year we get the top dozen leaders together once a week, for six to eight weeks. At the end of each of the weekly sessions, we have "homework" assignments to prepare for the next meeting. At the beginning of one session, a participant told us that at the last meeting he had offered to send us information which we had agreed to review and return with our comments. He went on to say that of the 12 messages he sent out, only three responses had been received. He then asked all of us what we were going to do about this issue of "irresponsibility." The meeting stopped and we discussed how to better honor our commitments. Right at the top of the organization's leadership, we are aware of the need to mirror whatever behavior we expect to receive in kind.

Schulze: When the Ritz-Carlton opened a new hotel or resort, I personally conducted seminars for all employees — from general manager to housekeeper. I began my presentation with these words: "I am president of Ritz-Carlton ... I am an important person." I would pause and then continue, "You are all important people too. You make this hotel run. If I am absent for a day, no one would notice. But you, ladies and gentlemen, would be missed. You make this company the best in the world."

At the Ritz-Carlton, we believe that employees, as well as guests, should be treated with respect and caring. The behavior of leaders should serve as daily examples. Often it is the small things that matter most. If I say that the organization respects and cares about employees, then it is inexcusable for me to pass any employee in the hallway without saying hello.

Leadership as Trust

Trust is the belief or confidence that one party has in the reliability, integrity and honesty of another party. It is the expectation that the faith one places in someone else or in some institution will be honored. These are difficult times for building trust. Skepticism is running high and many institutions once considered above reproach are now the subject of suspicion.

Trust is fragile, and building it isn't easy. But trust is the foundation of the leader/follower relationship. In high-trust environments, people are more willing to keep agreements, share information, admit and learn from mistakes, and take on greater responsibility. Trust must be visible and it must start at the top. Leaders have to be trusted — and to be trustworthy.

But trust is a two-way street. Encouraging workforce participation and responsibility requires a deep belief in the potential of your employees to make responsible decisions. And to prepare for making responsible decisions, people must be entrusted with information, resources, and support.

The issue of trust is also pivotal in a Living-Systems Model of organization, where leaders begin with a strong vision or intent — not a set of action plans — and expect plans to emerge locally from responses to the needs and contingencies inherent in that intent. In this model, it is crucial that leaders be able to trust the organization's intelligence and willingness to organize in whatever way the vision requires. Here's how some of the leaders I interviewed looked at the issue:

Coolidge: In the investment business, trust is everything. People trust us with their money, with handling transactions of significant magnitude, and with confidential information. Trust is fundamental to everything that we do. Just think about it: millions and millions of dollars are transacted with just a phone call. Trust permeates every transaction, so without a culture of trustworthiness, we're out of business. This means that leaders in our organization have to be people who are immensely trustworthy. Not only our clients, but also our employees, have to believe that leaders will make the right decision and do the right thing. And I think leaders engender trust by leading exemplary lives. They just have to be that way or else everything breaks down.

Crockett: Much of what brings people satisfaction in their jobs is the ability to make a difference, to create an impact, and to grow into their potential. If, as leaders, we're not able to trust the capability of our people, to trust that they understand our vision and where we're going, to trust in their skills and ability — then we are in big trouble. Risk-taking will come to a screeching halt and we're going to slow down productivity. Trust is the cornerstone of a strong corporate culture. It's important when things are going well — it's critical when times get tough. Our organizations have become so complex that one person can't oversee every decision —

trust is essential. If you don't trust them, talented people will leave for someplace where they *are* trusted.

Halloran: I have a deeply and fundamentally positive attitude about the worthiness of people to bring their very best to whatever challenge is at hand. It's not that I assume everybody's right all the time, but I always begin with the rock solid belief that everybody has a point of view that's worth hearing. Trust has to do with assuming that the other person has value to contribute, even before they've proven it. That's the core — the belief that people have value and that they are going to come up with good answers. So trust is most useful in the area of delegation. Unless I think that I can run my 1,000-person organization all by myself, I *have* to trust. I see trust as being highly practical.

Pieroni: The whole idea of delegation is based on trust. First of all, you must have the right people in place, but assuming that you do, you've got to give people the authority to do their jobs. That means you have to *trust* that they are willing and able to do their work and reach their goals.

Powell: You've got to be believed and you've got to be trusted. But, as a leader, you also have to trust others. Especially your direct reports. Delegation is all about trust. You can't delegate effectively as a leader unless you can trust people. A leadership lesson I learned early on was that I needed to figure out who I could trust to do the necessary tasks. So trust even goes beyond trusting a person to do the right thing, to be honest and work effectively. You also have to know who has the skills to get the job done.

Wikstrom: When we talk about trust at Reell, we use a pyramid model to display three elements: The base of the pyramid is HONESTY — the basic "don't lie, steal, cheat" ethic. The second tier is FAITHFULNESS — making and honoring commitments. And the top of the pyramid is COMPETENCE — confidence that someone has the ability to do what is required. (I may trust your honesty completely, and feel you are entirely faithful to your word, but if I need my appendix removed, I'm not going to trust you to do that task.) And trust always contains an element of time. You can't short-circuit the time it takes to build and maintain relational trust.

Dilenschneider: Any commercial interaction that we are engaged in has to be transcended by our personal relationship. So trust becomes terribly important.

Swenson: Getting people to place their trust in you is a matter of always doing what you say. One thing I've learned over the years is that you can talk until you're blue in the face, but you will never create trust unless your *sustained* behavior parallels what you say. This is why building trust takes so long. There has to be consistency over time. For example: My personal leadership style is to be candid, but because transparency is not the norm, people often think that I have another agenda. It takes time for them to realize that, with me, what you see is what you get.

Wittman: There is so much you ask of your team every day — especially in a difficult situation like bankruptcy — and if they don't trust how you're going to treat them and how you're going to make decisions, you can't be effective as a manager *let alone as* a leader. In dealing with the phenomenal teams I've been privileged to work with, I think I've gained their trust by being direct, candid and frank. It's all about building the right kinds of dialogue. They need to know you want both the good and the bad news as soon as they have it and have assessed it, and they need to know you will also share relevant information promptly. In those instances where you didn't share information fast enough, you have to have a defensible reason for it. And it can't just be that it was a hard conversation that you wanted to avoid.

Leadership as Vulnerability

Recognition of the potential of the workforce for contributing solutions to organizational problems has increased while once-assumed infallibility of leaders and the certainty of management decisions has declined. The unquestioned authority of leaders in the corporation of the past has been replaced by the need to acknowledge the expertise of those below, and to enlist employees as true partners. Moving from a model in which leadership made all the decisions and knew all the answers to an organizational environment of openness, candor and empowerment requires leaders to become and remain highly vulnerable.

There has never been a time in which our organizations have experienced more uncertainty and chaos. No one can predict the future and no one has all the answers. In this unpredictable business atmosphere, no decisions are permanent, not even the mission or core functions of the organization. Effective leaders don't promise to supply all the answers. Often, there is more that is unknown about the exact direction of the organization than is known — even at the highest levels. It may sound ironic, but the corporate leader who can say to his or her employees, "Sure, I'm scared too," will have done more for company morale with that single admission than a dozen phony pep talks ever could. Why? Because the candid sharing of vulnerabilities (as well as strengths) creates a sense of community in an organization and a sense of genuine value in each of its members. Here are some comments on how vulnerability can become a leadership strength:

Burnside: From my Center for Creative Leadership tenure, it became very clear that we all have great strengths and great weaknesses. What is very interesting, and a research-based truth, is that our great strengths usually create our weaknesses. It was always very tricky working with top leaders to say: "Keep your strength. It is a real asset, your main value, part of what made you successful. Now also develop the weakness that has developed from that strength."

I accept two things as a leader: 1) I am in the spotlight whether I like it or not. People are going to look at me and discuss my actions. And, because in senior leadership roles, I am carrying a fair amount of the weight of the organization, it's proper for people to discuss how I'm doing. And 2) If I can articulate my strengths and weaknesses to the organization, I believe that people will understand me as a leader who has integrity, who is trustworthy, and who will trust them — because I haven't positioned myself as some perfect being with all the answers. By making myself vulnerable in this way, I'm saying to people: "I'm a human being and I'm willing to hear from you how I might improve." I think that's very effective.

Coolidge: For us to succeed, we have to hire people who are superior performers — very smart, very motivated. The investment business attracts highly talented people. If you don't have intelligent, motivated employees at all levels, you are going to lose the strength of your organization. So you always have to hire people who are smarter and better than you. And obviously, for leaders, that can be risky. But you have to be willing to accept that risk of having strong people around you.

Our culture is very open, tolerant, and willing to accommodate the entrepreneurial thinker and try new things. For leaders to be open to criticism and receptive to new and different ideas might suggest weakness to some people. But to me it suggests strength. Only when you have a strong conviction in your own position and approach can you "take the heat" of criticism or really listen to the person who thinks we ought to be doing things differently.

Crockett: A former chairman of Allstate, Jerry Choate, took a huge risk when he stood up in front of a room full of people for a speech that was being broadcast to every employee. Not only did he introduce some important issues to the organization, he told a story about himself, his mother, how his mother had influenced him and what inspired him. Then he talked about his biggest fear. He said he was afraid that he could let us down. He said that by not being the right kind of CEO, he knew he could negatively impact, not only employees, but ultimately, the families of employees. And that's what kept him awake at night.

I've got to tell you, the feedback on that presentation was so powerful and meaningful that it startled me. I anticipated that the speech would get a positive reaction, but I was overwhelmed at the response. For Jerry to speak of what frightened him most — and to express that level of concern for each individual in the company — was extraordinarily compelling to our employees. That one speech did more for pulling our company together, for spring-boarding us into productivity goals and high levels of performance, than a hundred "motivational" talks ever could. That's what a leader has to be able to do. You have to be willing to reveal yourself.

Dilenschneider: Leaders have to be strong. They have to demonstrate by example that they have the skill (ability) and the will (desire) to do the job. If you have both the skill and the will, then, as a leader, you can afford to be vulnerable. And if you do it properly, it will inspire people around to pick up those parts of the challenge you're not prepared to deal with. I've seen that work in company after company. It's really all about team building. So, in that way, a leader can make his or her vulnerability a real asset. An example of someone who turned vulnerability into strength is Bill Agee, who used to run Bendix. Bill is a very able guy, but no one can know everything. He had a wonderful ability to bring people together, each one of whom felt, "I can help Bill because I have this specific talent and knowledge he lacks." People rallied to compensate for his "weaknesses," and Bill built an extraordinarily powerful team in that way.

Pieroni: I think that people will challenge any leader who states "here's where we're going!" before asking the question "where do you think we should be going?" A powerful leadership strategy is to allow the group to come to conclusions about what the challenges and solutions are. Even if you may know exactly where you want to go, you need to give people the opportunity to contribute to the overall shared goals and values.

It's often difficult for new managers to admit they don't have all the answers, that they can't address every question. People just coming into management or leadership positions sometimes don't have the confidence to admit their vulnerabilities and to say, "I don't know. I'd like to hear what you have to say."

Powell: As a leader, I always try to get people to tell me what they really think. I request this of my direct reports: "Part of your job is to tell me if you think I'm messing up. For example, if I say something in a speech to the staff, and you think it doesn't go over well, I want you to bring that to my attention." All people in leadership positions need that kind of honest reflection — somebody holding up a mirror so that you can see how you are really coming across. Everybody knows that no one is perfect. I want to relate to my direct reports and my staff very broadly. If you set yourself up on a pedestal, you don't connect with people. And, in the end, it's all about connecting with others.

These are confusing times for all of us, especially for those who are trying to make major decisions in a sea of change. No one leader can fully absorb and comprehend the colliding tyrannies of speed, quality, customer satisfaction, foreign competition, diversity and technology. By accepting and sharing imperfections, leaders show they are not afraid to admit they don't have all the answers — and that frees other people to admit that they don't have all the answers either. As Jack Welch once famously put it: "If you're not confused, you don't know what's going on."

Leadership as Values

Webster defines value as "a principle, standard or quality considered inherently worthwhile or desirable." The root is the Latin valor, which means strength. Values are a source of strength for an enterprise or an individual. As leadership strategy moves from coercion to cooperation, the key to bonding people to the goals of the organization automatically becomes the intangibles — relationships, commitments, shared values.

An organization with cohesive values is like a hologram — every part contains enough information in condensed form to describe the whole. A hologram is a wonderful image for an organization. An observer can see the whole organization's culture and ways of doing business by watching one individual — whether a production-floor employee, the receptionist at the front desk, or a senior manager. There is a consistency and predictability to their behavior. This quality is achieved through a combination of simply expressed expectations of acceptable behavior and the freedom available to individuals to align their actions with the boundaries of the whole organization's values.

A sales manager read an article about his company's refusal to deal with any country where "under the table" money was part of the negotiation process. He circled the article and wrote the words "Right On!" in the column, and mailed it to his CEO. Like the sales manager, many employees I've spoken with agree that they are happiest working where the values of their organizations reflect their own. Likewise, the leaders I interviewed were adamant that values played a critically important role in their organizations.

Coolidge: We've been a firm with a very consistent approach. Our name has never changed. We've never had a merger or acquisition. We've always emphasized employee continuity, as well as firm continuity. We've only had one form of organization — which is an independent employee-owned firm. This is all part of who we are.

The same is true for our values. When our industry changed, through consolidation with commercial banks and other large financial institutions, there was a corresponding shift of focus away from serving investors to providing the most capital and doing the biggest deal. In our organization, investor interests have always remained primary. Obviously, we have to be flexible and entrepreneurial, and always figure out what it takes to be successful in different environments — but the fundamental principles and values are set. After 68 years, people understand that we are in business for the long haul.

William Blair & Company

Our Mission Is To Achieve Success For Our Clients

We Believe:

That our time, energy, and resources should be committed to our clients' success…

That relationships with clients and prospects are valuable and should be nurtured, developed, and never taken for granted…

That our employee ownership and independence make us a unique provider of objective advice…

That the people of William Blair & Company are our firm's most valuable resource…

That quality — of our service and our results — is essential to achieving success…

That our performance is based on professional experience, industry knowledge, hard work, and integrity…

That our focus on growth and emerging companies and the middle market differentiates us from our large competitors…

That the firm's financial success and profitability allow us to further invest in helping our clients succeed…

That community involvement, through financial support and volunteer service, is part of our culture, heritage, and reputation…

Feldt: As we created our vision, we also defined the beliefs that underlie the vision. When you visit our New York headquarters, you'll see our beliefs statement displayed as you walk in the front door. Every floor of this building has at least one of our beliefs written on the wall, and beside the statement is a display of photos and videos that exemplify our values and beliefs. In a mission-driven organization like Planned Parenthood, we wear our values on our sleeves every day. Our work is all about living our mission. And leaders in this organization are especially scrutinized to make sure that our actions are congruent with what we say we believe.

THE PLANNED PARENTHOOD BELIEFS

We believe in the right to sexual and reproductive self-determination that is non-coercive, non-exploitive, and responsible.

We believe that the free and joyous expression of one's own sexuality is central to being fully human.

We believe in trusting individuals and providing them with the information they need to make well-informed decisions about sexuality, family planning, and childbearing.

We believe that women should have an equal place at life's table, and be respected as moral decision makers.

We believe that children flourish best in families and communities where they are nurtured, honored, and loved.

We believe in passion — for change, for justice, for easing the plight of others, for caring, for living our convictions, and for confronting inhumane acts.

We believe in action — to make things happen and to improve people's lives and circumstances.

We believe in inclusion and diversity — and the power and knowledge they confer.

We believe the future is global and that we are part of a global movement.

We believe in the urgency of creating a sustainable world and living in peace with our planet.

We believe in leadership based upon collaboration rather than hierarchy.

We believe in acting courageously, especially as allies with those who have little or no voice and little or no power.

We believe that every right is tied to responsibility and that the fulfillment of responsibility is itself a source of joy.

Halloran: Whether they are established deliberately or by accident, communities of people create a set of values. Sometimes these values are created by default, and sometimes they are the unhappy result of poorly chosen decisions and actions. But values are never *not* present. So given that they are going to be part of your company, regardless, why not try to create the healthiest possible values? Companies and organizations vary enormously on how much energy and creativity members are willing to volunteer in pursuit of their joint goals. And a lot of that variation has to do with not just the tasks, measures, outputs and results. It has to do with values that are expressed in daily actions. Do people feel they are part of something worth doing? Do they feel valued and recognized? Do they see how what they are doing fits into the larger whole? If not, your organization is going to be at a disadvantage.

AGILENT'S VALUES

Innovation and contribution
Trust, respect, and teamwork
Uncompromising integrity

Focus

Speed

Accountability

Hefner: Values — regardless of whether or not they are formally stated — are important in all organizations. It is foolish for any leader *not* to recognize how much people are influenced by the values of a company's culture.

PLAYBOY'S VALUES

- Stay close to the market
- Create products of the highest quality and value with lead pricing
- Operate with a sense of urgency
- Take ownership for our products and the company
- Decentralize decision-making
- Foster a "let's try it" attitude
- Respect the dignity of individuals
- Invest in training, build careers
- Encourage a "have fun" environment

Schulze: Values (the philosophy and practices) are the heart and soul of our organization. The sign outside means nothing if the heart and soul are not in it. It is not enough for people just to fill functions. They have to know what we are all about.

Leaders must stay focused on values and keep them energized — which is the hardest part. For that, you need to find processes that renew and reenergize values. One process that Ritz-Carlton uses is called the "Line Up." Fifteen minutes before a shift begins every day, the leader of the line up goes through the basics of that day. Employees of R-C all over the world are reminded of the same "value of the day," as prepared by the corporate office. Added to that is a "teaching" — an issue brought to our awareness, based on customer-service input, and then some comments about the daily value that are customized to the individual hotel.

THE RITZ-CARLTON CREDO

The Ritz-Carlton is a place where the genuine care and comfort of our guests is our highest mission.

We pledge to provide the finest personal service and facilities for our guests who will always enjoy a warm, relaxed yet refined ambience.

The Ritz-Carlton experience enlivens the senses, instills well-being, and fulfills even the unexpressed wishes and needs of our guests.

Our motto is: We are Ladies and Gentlemen serving Ladies and Gentlemen.

Smith: Corporate values are the reinforcing mechanism for the achievement of objectives. For example, if our vision is to become the best express company in the world, then our values — the way we treat people, the high service standards we set — become reinforcement for reaching that goal.

FEDERAL EXPRESS' CORPORATE PHILOSOPHY

From its inception Federal Express has put people first both because it is right to do so and because it is good business as well. Our corporate philosophy is succinctly stated: People-Service-Profit.

Wikstrom: The three founders of Reell share many basic convictions about the importance of balancing work and family responsibilities and the need to practice ethical principles in the workplace. Our values reflect a willingness to place the well-being of employees and their families above unfettered profit growth, and a commitment to doing what is right even when it doesn't seem profitable, expedient or conventional.

REELL PRECISION MANUFACTURING CORPORATION

Reell is a team dedicated to the purpose of operating a business based on the practical application of Judeo-Christian values for the mutual benefit of **co-workers and their families, customers, shareholders, suppliers, and community.** We are committed to provide an environment where there is harmony between work and our moral/ethical values and family responsibilities and where everyone is treated justly.

DO WHAT IS RIGHT We are committed to do what is right even when it does not seem to be profitable, expedient, or conventional.

DO OUR BEST In our understanding of excellence we embrace a commitment to continuous improvement in everything we do. It is our commitment to encourage, teach, equip and free each other to do and become all that we were intended to be.

TREAT OTHERS AS WE WOULD LIKE TO BE TREATED

SEEK INSPIRATIONAL WISDOM by looking outside ourselves, especially with respect to decisions having far-reaching and unpredictable consequences, but we will act only when action is confirmed unanimously by others concerned.

Wittman: One of the incidents that made me feel like I'd completely hit the jackpot by joining Adelphia happened in the third or fourth week after I started with the company. I attended a leadership meeting for our top 25–30 people where Ron Cooper, the chief operating officer, spent three-quarters of a day talking about Adelphia's new mission statement and values. Afterward, we went into breakout sessions to debate, challenge, rearrange, and edit what he had presented. Then Ron spent the next two months traveling around the country, getting together with 80 percent of our 14,000 employees, face to face, to talk about these values. That was stunning to me. Generally, I am a cynic. But I remember sitting in that conference room in Virginia, soaking it all up like a sponge. I was starved for this kind of thinking.

ADELPHIA'S VALUES

- Urgency
- Accountability
- Integrity
- Respect
- Ethical Conduct
- Teamwork and Communication
- Recognition and Celebration

Values written on a plaque or laminated card are meaningless. (This is where you may start, but it is only a beginning.) They must be integrated into processes, policies, and organizational behavior. Values become real when they offer a shared understanding to "how we do things around here."

Adelphia COO Ron Cooper agrees: "You've got to move values from being theoretical or aspirational into something that's very tangible. When we say one of our values is urgency, what are the specific behaviors that would be tangible evidence of those values in action? When we were addressing groups all across the company, we tried to use generic examples of behaviors. For instance, on the value of urgency, we talked about fact-gathering, decision-making, and doing that at a pace that was quite different from Adelphia's historical pace. We talked about how urgency ties into responsiveness to colleagues, to customers and to various other constituents by showing that we take their concerns seriously, that they are valuable to us."

Various leaders at Adelphia took these same values back to their departments to discuss what actions they felt best supported the values. For example, David Brunick and his team in human resources looked at the behaviors specific to HR that they had to demonstrate and live in order to be a model for the organization. David said, "That exercise made the values a little more real in how they affect our job day to day." Here is an outline of what his department concluded:

Supporting Adelphia's Values

Urgency — respond within 48 hours

Accountability — make decisions, take responsibility, share learning

Integrity — tell it like it is, keep commitments

Respect — gain input before acting, accept differences, be respectful

Ethical Conduct — lead by example, support each other, enforce feedback, ensure compliance

Teamwork and Communication — regular and effective information-sharing in/out of HR, arrive at solutions together, reach out to others

Recognition and Celebration — reward our values, set performance-based goals, recognize accomplishments, say "thanks" every day

Leadership as Motivation

The secret to being a great motivator is knowing that motivation cannot be forced or ordered. Motivation is an intrinsic human characteristic that can be tapped, nurtured and developed — but never coerced. In essence, all motivation is *self-motivation*. It manifests when leaders hold a compelling vision of the future, have a strong personal desire to realize the vision and possess the ability to encourage other people to do the same..

To be effective motivators, leaders must have insight into the human heart and sensitivity toward the hopes and aspirations of others. When the renowned Broadway director and choreographer Bob Fosse died, reporters commented on the immense loyalty his performers always showed. One dancer summed it up for everyone when she said: "We always knew that whatever Bob asked us to do — even if it was difficult or felt awkward — it was to make us look good."

A manager at a utilities company had a similar experience with a leader in her career: "We knew he wanted us to succeed. He was always acknowledging our good work and at the same time, always pushing us to improve. He had an almost *magical* ability to urge us to excel in ways that never trivialized our current achievements." Memorable leaders inspire exceptional levels of commitment and performance.

Burnside: When I was at Wrangler Brand Apparel, I worked for a leader who was very motivational. My boss there was Robert M. O'Dear. I always felt that he absolutely trusted me when he gave me assignments. Essentially, he sized up who he had on his team, and then decided who was best to get the job done. When he picked assignments for me, he also took responsibility for having chosen me. He gave me absolute freedom to succeed or fail, but I always felt supported by this man. With the assurance of both his trust and his commitment, I felt that whether I won or lost, he was with me. It was extremely motivating working for Robert O'Dear. I gave that job everything I had.

Coolidge: When I interviewed for the firm, Edward Blair (son of the founder) was the managing partner. I asked a typical business-school graduate question of Mr. Blair: "What's your vision of the firm for the long term?" And he answered, "My job is to make sure the firm survives beyond the family, and that we bring in the kind of people who can take it over." So I thought to myself, "Okay! There's a chance for me." Mr. Blair stated that his goal was to turn the firm over to the best and the brightest. That's a great motivator! And I think that is still a motivator for our current "best and brightest." Virtually everybody who is on the professional side knows that maybe some day, they won't just be doing the deals or managing the portfolios or working in the brokerage side. They could end up as a member of the leadership team. That's the commitment I've made to them: "We are going to remain independent and promote from within our own ranks." That was what was done for me, and that's what I'm going to do. My job is to hand a strong firm to the next generation.

Crockett: Two key ingredients — the right people and the right motivation — fuel high performance. Motivation shows up in lots of different ways. It is a very personal and individual thing. I was at a claim office of about 125 employees, walking through the office with the claim manager. This particular manager had received fantastic feedback on our Quality Leadership Measurement System (QLMS) survey, so I was curious to watch her with her people to figure out what generated not only the good financial results, but also this great feedback. And as we walked through the room, conversing about the normal work conditions, she would often stop and refer to specific individuals: "Steve over there has been in our area for 15 years. Steve also coaches Little League. How was the game on Thursday, Steve? Great! You won another one. He's got a winning record this year, Joan." We'd then move on to someone else, and as we left that person's area, quietly the claim manager would say, "Sally had some problems with her daughter this year. She's a teenager, you know. And these are tough years. We've had many sessions behind closed doors where she's trying to sort through these problems."

It became apparent to me that this woman knew all of her people. And I don't mean just knew their jobs. She knew each individual — what their concerns were, what got them excited. She knew when they were upbeat because things were going well, and she knew when they were struggling and needed her time and attention. When I asked, "How on earth can you do this for 125 people?" she replied, "That's my job."

This kind of motivation is hard work. And I think a lot of people want to simplify it. They want to assume motivation is all about monetary rewards, a formal recognition program, a once-a-month pat on the back, or a little feedback now and then. But it's so much more than that.

Motivation has as many different faces as the employees being led. There's no one-size-fits-all. Motivation is really about the daily encouragement and support that only happens when you understand and embrace employees at the human level.

Dilenschneider: Barney Clarke, the CEO of Columbia Gas Systems, was brilliant — a genius who thought *way* outside the box. Although I suspect he had the answers all the time, he spent hours talking with us, involving us and making us feel as if we were an integral part of a huge change — as if we were making history. And he got so much out of all of us. We'd work 'round the clock. Working with Barney was exciting, exhausting, incredibly intense and absolutely thrilling.

Feldt: I am so goal-oriented, and such a self-starter, that I have problems understanding that all people aren't like me in this regard. But I've learned a lot about motivation by observing certain affiliate CEOs, and seeing how they work with their staff. The best of these leaders connect with people in a way that makes their staff want to do a really good job *because of* that personal connection, affection, and respect. These CEOs give people the opportunity to take on tasks that may be a little bit above them, give them a lot of support and encouragement, and allow them to learn from their failures as well as their successes.

Halloran: Working with my current boss, Ned Barnholt, the CEO of Agilent is highly motivating. He and I have exactly aligned values and we share the same high aspirations about wanting to make this company a truly great place for people to work for the long term. How many vice presidents of Human Resources could be so lucky as to have the hope of building this kind of support in a boss? Not many! And here I am with as much runway as I need to take this somewhere. It's all about Ned's aspirations for the kind of company he wants to create — and his confidence and expectation that I can contribute to that.

Pieroni: It all starts with creating a vision that people can rally around. Without a powerful focal point, it is difficult to release an organization's motivation. That said — the leaders I recall as the most motivational were also the ones who were "in the boat" with you. They didn't stay above the job or the project or the exercise or the problem. Instead, they became part of the team, working together to find solutions to "our" challenges.

Smith: Employees must have a minimal level of skills in order to do a particular job. Leaders must be able to motivate people from the low end of the performance spectrum (doing the least amount possible without getting fired) toward the end of the spectrum where people consistently do the best job possible. One of the best leaders I ever had was my staff sergeant in the Marine Corps. He embodied the characteristics of true leadership and made us want to give our very best *every* day on *every* assignment.

Swenson: The best leader I ever worked for, Lee Cox of Pacific Telesis, combined the ability to understand organizational dynamics with an exceptional ability to deal with people. At meetings he would pose questions that left us curious, energized, and motivated. We couldn't do enough for him. Sometimes I wondered if we

were all hypnotized. I've never seen people work so hard for someone and still want to do more.

FROM MANAGEMENT TO LEADERSHIP

Several management experts have noted that American organizations are over-managed and under-led. If this is an accurate
observation about your organization, then now is the time to correct the imbalance. You might be able to manage stability, but you
must have leadership during transitions. While many of the leaders I interviewed made clear distinctions between the skills of management and the spirit of leadership, others commented how the
two need to blend:

Burnside: Regardless of who does the research, two factors
always come up when studying leadership: relationships and tasks.
Essentially, management is more about the task side of leadership
— arranging resources, putting the staff together, making sure
we've got the right amount of time and money, and getting things
done from a task standpoint. The relationship side is what we traditionally think of as leadership. It encompasses effectiveness in
interpersonal relationships with team members and with others.
But the point I want to make is that both of these factors have to be
utilized in ways that move an organization toward an objective
that is of value. Who wants a leader who can't manage? Who wants
a manager who can't lead? Leadership and management are integrated — and we need to think of them in an integrated way.

Dilenschneider: Managers focus on what is happening.
Leaders focus on what is *possible.* Managers are process-oriented,
they make the gears mesh and the trains run on time — and this is
important because most leaders can't do it. Leaders inspire people
to higher levels of achievement. They generate ownership and pride.

Halloran: Leaders and managers are both very important, but
they're not the same at all. You can get the sense of the differences

by looking at the etymology of the two words. *Manage* comes to English from an old Italian word "maneggiare," that literally means "to control a horse." It's about the process of training a horse by putting your hands on it. Whereas *lead* comes from an old English word which means "he who goes first in battle." It's a military term for the person whose role is pathfinder. Leading doesn't have anything to do with controlling or managing. I don't even think of those two concepts together anymore. Leaders are the pathfinders who go first. Managers control or support what already is established.

Pieroni: Managers are basically in a supervisory role: they give people assignments, follow up and make sure things get done. Leadership goes far beyond that. Leaders are strategic, visionary, motivating — all the things we've already talked about. But, most of all, leaders are role models. The moment you are in a senior management position, whether you like it or not, you are a role model. When you walk down the hall, people are judging you, saying either: "I can see how that person was given leadership responsibility" or "How did a person like *that* ever get into a leadership position?" I tell new leaders, "As you come to work each and every day, you are a role model — either a good one or a bad one. People you work with are noticing how you dress, how you act, how you treat people, how you make decisions, whether or not you are accessible, and how you manage others. If you really think of yourself as a role model in your work environment — then *everything* you do matters.

Smith: Management is the analytical science of ascertaining what the organization needs to do in order to become more successful and efficient. Managers utilize quantitative tools and skills. Leadership is the process of coalescing a group of individual activities and efforts toward not just individual, but organizational goals. Leaders need to have tremendous personal commitment to the vision and the ability to enlist support from others.

Swenson: I see management and leadership as intertwined. Management is about results, and leadership is about vision. Management is concerned with the day-to-day results that eventually deliver a plan. Leadership is about creating that plan: It is about creating the vision and developing the organization to support the vision.

Wikstrom: It has been said that you manage *things* and lead *people.* I think we are moving toward a manager/leader hybrid. You have to be effective organizing and managing tasks, but almost always those tasks are carried out by other people.

Wittman: There are a ton of good managers, and some have leadership qualities. Good managers reach their goals and motivate their teams. But if you are a leader, your influence goes beyond your direct reports and your job description. If people from other parts of the organization look to you for comments and insights, if your reaction to good news or bad news affects a wide range of people, if your thoughts about how to solve problems resonate with other people — then you are a leader.

In general, managers deal with processes, programs and projects. Leaders provide people with vision and build organizational energy. They create a sense of teamwork — you work *with* leaders, not *for* them. Management has to do with the here and now — work flow, processes and resources. Leadership is more future-focused and visionary. It requires risk-taking, out-of-the-box thinking, and creating a supportive environment in which people can truly develop their potential.

Contrary to several of the panel members, I rarely see this as an either/or issue. In today's business world, we have to work at being good at both management and leadership. But there is a point in your career when you have increased responsibility for other people's success. At this point, you'll need to spend the most time developing your leadership abilities.

TRANSFORMING MANAGERS INTO LEADERS

From Manager	To Leader
Uses power to persuade others	Shares power and responsibility
Expected to know the right answer	Initiates search for multiple right answers
Hands-on involvement	Self-directed teams
Gains compliance	Builds commitment
Enforces rules	Presents clear choices
Punishes failure	Encourages and analyzes failure
Takes success for granted	Celebrates and analyzes success
Protects people from negativity	Communicates candidly
Motivates through "pep" talks	Builds climate for self-motivation
Builds dependence	Develops new leaders
Sets goals for others	Inspires people to set and reach their own high goals and standards
Controls and commands	Liberates potential
Expects loyalty	Encourages mutual loyalty
Communicates in words	Communicates through congruent words and actions
Process-oriented	People-oriented
Focuses on present task	Focuses on future possibilities
Thinks incrementally	Thinks in discontinuous leaps

DEVELOPING FUTURE LEADERS

In today's "knowledge work" — with its reliance on project teams and cross-functional collaboration — leadership in peer relationships is becoming increasingly important. As the guidance of team efforts tends to shift to whoever has the needed information or expertise, more people in the organization must be able to assume the role of leader. More than ever before, successful corporations can't just wait for leaders to emerge, fully developed. They must actively seek out people with leadership potential and find ways to nurture and develop that potential.

Burnside: Ketchum's succession planning process relies on senior level executives identifying individuals who are among our top talent. Then those individuals are given assignments to help them grow and develop. An example is the head of our brand practice, also the associate director of our New York office, who recently took an assignment as director of the Atlanta office as a way of rounding out her expertise. That was a decision made to advance her career, and looked at from the standpoint of what would add the most value for her. Another example is the director of our San Francisco office, who took on the leadership of our London office, so that he could gain international experience.

Leadership potential at Ketchum is a combination of three factors: 1) The individual is a good reflection of the agency's values and culture. Our values are similar to a lot of other organizations (honesty, respect, teamwork, initiative, passion, precision), but we are looking to see if this person actually lives out the values in his or her behaviors. 2) The individual is a good example of delivery of services to clients (including being successful in the revenue side). 3) The individual is respected by and develops the people for whom he or she has leadership responsibility. To make the top list, you have to be hitting on all three cylinders.

Coolidge: All of our leaders, department managers, and CEOs have come from within the organization. We hire people (some with experience, and some right out of school) to work in the professional ranks of deal-doers, money-managers, brokers. Over time, we get to know them quite well. If they succeed in their area, they become partners or principals in the firm.

In our industry, we tend to promote big producers. There is some criticism of this practice — and rightfully so. Not every successful banker or broker makes a great manager. But in our culture, in order to command the respect of the troops, you have to have "been there and done it." People who work for you need to know that you understand what they are going through, and that you know what it takes to succeed. And virtually all of our leaders continue to be client-service people even after they assume the department manager job — or even the role of chief executive officer.

Crockett: At Allstate, developing new leadership is something that all current leaders are responsible for, and we use a systematic approach. It takes a serious commitment of both time and resources to do it right. But it is the key to what separates great companies from good companies. Great companies make developing leaders a priority.

The commitment has to start at the top, and Ed Liddy, our CEO, spends a great deal of his time focused on this issue — assessing leadership strengths, our current and future needs, and who's coming up. We start with the early identification of the high potentials. And I do mean early. Ten or 15 years before we expect a person to be at their full potential, our leadership councils are discussing how to develop this individual.

A good development plan comes from understanding both the leader's strengths — and how they can be leveraged — and where the person needs to develop. Since most learning comes from experience, we're not just talking about giving someone classroom training. Of course, that may be part of it. The most valuable conversation will be around how people use their time. How can their skills be leveraged in new ways? Who needs to know these people? Who should be working with them, coaching and mentoring them? What assignments and projects should they be given? What experiences do they need? There are inherent risks in the development process that have to be managed. The individual takes the risk of leaving the familiar and the business unit takes the risk of taking on an unknown in a key assignment.

It's important that leadership development not be viewed as a once-a-year event — it's work that good leaders do every day.

Dilenschneider: Future leaders need to be mentally prepared for the task of being a leader. This starts with developing an ability to think outside the box by constantly asking "What if ... ?"

and developing plans around a variety of possible scenarios. But the most important mental preparation for leadership is to learn how to keep a sense of perspective through the heights of successes and the depths of failure and setbacks by understanding that in both cases: "This too shall pass." Keeping your balance at all times can be extremely difficult since leaders play the game at the highest and lowest levels — they experience the glory of the victories as well as the shock and disappointment that also comes with the territory. The trick is not to let the glory go to your head nor let the disappointments devastate you. Future leaders are developed by giving people the freedom to succeed and fail, and the guidance to help them deal with both.

Hefner: At Playboy, we empower and encourage people throughout the enterprise to identify those who have leadership potential. Then we offer a leadership development program to acknowledge and develop that potential. Employees who want to be leaders here need to realize that leadership is *not* about having a large number of people reporting to you or even wearing the title of executive. Leaders are the *influencers* in an organization — and any employee's current relationships, interactions, and reputation afford great opportunities to demonstrate leadership abilities.

Pieroni: Leadership organically emerges under certain circumstances, and if you keep your eyes open, you'll see it demonstrated. In an area of complex problems or in times of crisis, there are people who rise to the top. They are proactive, reliable, thoughtful, and they automatically take control. These natural leaders speak up — and other people listen to them because they're providing solutions, not just stating problems. I've seen it here at Sankyo. Every time we are in a tough situation, people point to the same two or three individuals because we feel confident these "leaders" will go well beyond their area of responsibility — and do whatever is needed.

Powell: You need to identify people who have a "spark," an aptitude for being leaders. Then you need to provide them with good training, with assignments that allow them to grow and with the mentoring that helps them grow. It's critical to have all three. And what goes hand in hand with that is succession planning. I come into an organization as a change-agent, and tend to stay for 3–5 years. So, as soon as I take a job, I start looking for people who can be groomed as my successor. Having a well-thought-out succession-planning program in any organization is very important. And definitive, purposeful success planning is rare, even at the very highest corporate levels.

Schulze: We have a leadership profile taken from our top leaders that we use to identify candidates who have the highest potential for leadership. We are looking for those who have the ability to live in accordance with our values. And, in general, we have found that among the most successful leadership qualities are a genuine caring about people and the ability to develop interpersonal relationships.

Smith: We found out long ago that people need to have certain identifiable traits in order to be effective as leaders in our environment at Federal Express. Our Leadership Evaluation and Awareness Program begins by employees identifying themselves as candidates and expressing a desire for the company to prepare them for management/leadership positions. These employees participate in a process that explains the demands of management as well as the personal characteristics and traits needed for successful leadership. I find it interesting that, once they know the demands and requirements, some 70 percent of the participants drop out of the program.

Swenson: Here is how I describe the importance of developing future leaders: Everybody wants to win the Super Bowl, but you can't win it with the Junior Varsity team. If you don't have people who are thinking through business challenges and coming up with their own initiatives and are developing their own people, your organization is going to hit a wall sooner or later.

Wikstrom: At Reell, work directors (supervisors) are called "advisors." While every employee has only one advisor, the advisors may have as many as three or four "advisees." Beyond the particular functions of his or her job, advisors take on the role of developing their advisees. In this way, leadership is continually encouraged and developed on a one-on-one basis.

Leadership development isn't just an organizational issue. It's also the responsibility of the individual. Some words of advice for future leaders:

Powell: I was not a leader in high school. I didn't develop leadership skills until I was in college — and other people noticed it before I did. When I was a sophomore, the chemistry department at the University of Maryland chose me to represent them on a faculty committee. And then, in my sorority, people asked if I would consider being president.

Often, somebody will ask you to accept a challenge, and it may not come at the most convenient time for you. You may even be concerned about whether you have the capabilities needed. My advice is to stop and think again. The person who asked you to take on the assignment sees something in you that you may not see in yourself. So if you think you might be able to stretch and go for it — do so when the opportunity is there. They might not ask a second time.

Dilenschneider: People need to recognize that there are two paths in life: The first is to be a fine, upstanding person who never pushes him or herself to play the game at higher levels. And this is a good choice — perhaps a safer choice. But if you believe, as I do, that we are on the earth for a short period of time, and that the purpose of life is to discover our gifts and utilize them to the best of our abilities — then if you *don't* try to play the game, you will never fully realize your potential.

Unquestionably true. Realizing full potential is the ultimate goal — and not only for leaders. Tapping the maximum potential of the entire workforce must be the objective for all enterprises — and enlightened leadership is only half the battle. Most modern businesses, however liberated their corporate philosophies, are still three-dimensional structures with strong vertical components in which the majority of players remain formally subordinate to the people who hire, train and reward them. For any organization to make real progress toward the fully interactive, Living-System Model called for in the new business age, it must also rethink its "compact" — the relationship existing between employer and employee. Chapter Six examines the dilemma of the inherited hierarchical business structure and considers ways to "level the playing field" so that people throughout the organization can start seeing themselves as equal participants in a cause shared by all.

CHAPTER 6

THE LOYALTY FACTOR

"This isn't the deal I signed up for."

"The fundamental premise of the new model executive ... is, simply, that the goals of the individual and the goals of the organization will work out to be the same. These young men have no cynicism about 'the system,' and little skepticism. ... They have an implicit faith that The Organization will be as interested in making use of their best qualities as they are themselves, and thus, with equanimity, they can entrust the resolution of their destiny to The Organization. ... the average young man cherishes the idea that his relationship with The Organization is to be for keeps."

William H. Whyte, Jr.,
***The Organization Man* (1956)**

YOU WENT TO SCHOOL, you acquired marketable skills, and you got a job. You worked hard, contributing your time and energy to the organization you joined. You made personal sacrifices for your job, some at the expense of your family. In return, your grateful company rewarded you with job security, incremental raises and promotions based on length of tenure in the "corporate family." And after 30 or 40 years with your

Industrial Age organization, you retired with a comfortable pension and the congratulations of your boss and colleagues.

In the "old deal" employer-employee compact described above, workers were guaranteed job security in a safe, stable organization. Factory giants protected their workers by offering fair compensation and lifetime security. Sometimes as part of this social compact, employers provided subsidized housing near the factory site. In the spirit of this paternalistic relationship, Americans referred to their employers by nicknames: Bell Telephone was "Ma Bell," Pillsbury was "Mother Pillsbury," and Kodak was "The Great Yellow Father." And in return for the benefits of paternalism, employees were expected to be totally loyal. They stayed with one company for the length of their careers, followed orders without challenging the status quo, did good work and supported the positions of their organizations both privately and in public.

THE CHALLENGE OF TRANSITION

David Brunick, senior vice president of Human Resources at Adelphia Communications, talked with me about the challenge of moving an organization from the old to the new deal: "The people who are here today signed up for a business that was very paternalistic. For them the deal was: Maybe I don't get to make a lot of decisions, maybe I don't like the way things get done here, and maybe I don't have much influence or authority — but if I show up every day for work, the family will make sure I'm taken care of. (And, in this case, it was literally a family-operated and -led company.) So the shift we're now making is from 'loyalty to family' to 'commitment to business success.' And that's a very different deal. For some people, it's great. It's almost like being set free from prison: very exciting, very inspiring. They 'get it' immediately. They understand that if we have a business that thrives, it means opportunity and success for employees. But we also have people at the other end of the continuum who are frightened by the changes in strategy and culture. I've kept people in HR who are very excited by the new deal, and those in the middle whose attitude is, 'I'd like to like it, but I'm not sure yet.' I also had to separate about 25 percent of the team. That's sad and unfortunate. But when you need to change a culture quickly, and you've done a good job of articulating where you're headed, and given people time to try out the new behaviors, then you need to gauge their reactions. You will see some who feel, 'This isn't the deal I signed on for. I don't like it, and I never will,' and with those people you have to cut ties."

Many employees I interviewed were struggling with the transition from the old deal to the new. It seemed to them as though the balance had tilted in favor of the employer, and that the company had abandoned its responsibility to them. People felt they had traded a paternalistic relationship for a one-sided loyalty in which they were expected to work harder than ever in an atmosphere of confusion and impermanence, without having their concerns acknowledged or their efforts adequately rewarded.

When the compact feels heavily weighted to the advantage of employers, the natural tendency of employees is to withdraw their loyalty and commitment. The paradoxical result is that as organizations strive to reinvigorate workforce spirit, employees grow steadily more passive, acting upon new directives and directions, but without committing to the goals underlying them. The fact that so many workers had this negative perception about the current state of their relationship with their employers points to the difficulty we are all having trying to make the transition from the traditional to the new workplace.

LOYALTY REDEFINED

Loyalty has two dimensions: the internal or emotional level and the external, behavioral aspect. Internally, loyalty is a feeling of bonding, mutuality, affiliation and caring. Various dictionaries define loyalty as "true, constant or steadfast in allegiance." One definition is "faithful to a person, ideal, custom, obligation, duty or organization." Another definition is "devoted attachment and affection." For our purposes, the key to defining loyalty starts here: *Loyalty is first of all an emotion that is experienced internally as caring, concern and feeling of responsibility for another person or entity.* Loyalty is basic to our nature as human beings — a potent force that can be brought forth for the good of all.

In his book, *Passions Within Reason: The Strategic Role of the Emotions,* Cornell University professor Robert H. Frank states that emotions are not just the "fuzzy thinking" that most other economists believe them to be. "Rather," he says, "emotions serve a highly useful function. They short-circuit some types of self-interested behavior by bonding people to external projects, to beliefs, and to relationships that are not always in the individual's narrow self-interest. Emotions cause people to feel strongly about things outside themselves."

But since emotions are intangible, it is almost always through the behavioral dimension that we evaluate another's loyalty to us. In organizations we often have expectations of loyal behavior that are implied rather then explicit. Therefore, employers and employees alike need to understand the changing dynamics of organizational loyalty, and how to apply that understanding in the workplace to create bonds that will serve them in the future. It is not only the employer who has developed new definitions of loyalty, the workforce has too.

In the past, employee loyalty to a company was synonymous with following orders and not questioning authority. In contrast, today's most loyal workers speak up to identify problems and implement improvements. To a traditional manager who still equates loyalty with blind obedience, employee criticism may be interpreted as arrogant or interfering. But to the more aware employer, active involvement is seen as a positive expression of commitment: People speak up because they care about what happens to this company.

Loyalty can no longer be equated to length of service, either. Especially in the new workforce. Flying from Washington, D.C. to San Francisco, I sat next to Laura, a highly regarded human resource specialist in her late 20s. She told me that during an interview for a management position, she had been asked a standard interview question: "Where do you see yourself within this company in 10 years?"

"I don't think I made a very good impression," Laura said. "I told them that I didn't see myself staying with *any* company for the next 10 years." Nonetheless, Laura believes she is a loyal employee. According to her: "I've always chosen to work at a company where I could be loyal to my employer. I show my loyalty by working hard, being extremely dedicated and honest, and by contributing far beyond my job description. It's just that I'm more interested in developing my abilities than I am staying with one organization forever."

LOYALTY AND RESTRUCTURING

Frank was a loyal employee at a *Fortune* 500 company, a man on the "fast track" according to his envious peers. When the company began restructuring, Frank's career stalled. He was moved from a line management position into a staff function, and was finally assigned to an organizational task force. Feeling that his talents weren't being utilized, Frank's morale plummeted: "I never thought I'd feel this way. I used to come to work 'all fired up.' Now I simply put in my time. How am I supposed to care about what happens to the company when it doesn't care about me?" Six months later, Frank left to join another firm.

In contrast, Samantha's loyalty to her company was actually strengthened during a downsizing: "Last year we found that our entire department was going to be eliminated. At a time of corporate-wide cutbacks, my boss helped all of us relocate to other jobs within the company. She really went to bat for us. She set up interviews with different department heads, checked later for feedback on how well we did, and once I even heard her on the telephone saying, 'Well, could you try him anyway? He doesn't make a very good first impression, but I promise you he can do the job.' How loyal am I to this organization? *Very* loyal!"

Even though everyone knows that restructuring can lead to layoffs in today's business reality, employees still report plunging loyalty when layoffs are handled badly: "The focus is all on stockholders and the bottom line. Decisions seem to be made solely from a financial perspective with no concern for people. In cutting jobs, there has been no loyalty shown to those who've been here the longest or done the best work."

When it comes to massive downsizing, responsible employers show loyalty by taking a long-term view of employment. This doesn't mean they guarantee jobs for life, or fail to remove underperforming employees, or disregard profit and shareholders. It just means that employers tell their people what's happening, do their best to keep employees who are performing well in their jobs — and use layoffs only as a last resort.

LOYALTY PRINCIPLES

As a leader, you cannot afford to remain uninformed regarding the changing dynamics of organizational loyalty. To do so is to risk making costly mistakes with your workforce. The loyalty issue has traditionally been an unconscious part of employment agreements. To examine the implications of changing organizational loyalty, it is necessary to develop a conscious awareness of the process. The following principles will be useful:

Loyalty Principle #1:
Loyalty begins when one party genuinely cares about another.

Loyalty starts with a sincere intent to do your best on someone else's behalf. To obtain ongoing loyalty, participants must believe that each party has a genuine concern for the well-being of the other. Jim Nordstrom, the former CEO of Nordstrom, says: "It's no great trick getting people to be loyal. Folks will be almost embarrassingly loyal to anyone who genuinely cares about them."

Loyalty Principle #2: For loyalty to thrive in a relationship, it must be mutual and be perceived as mutual.

Since loyalty is both an emotional state of mind and a behavior pattern, and since people judge the internal emotion by the external manifestation, your actions must be perceived to be caring by those whose loyalty you seek to engage.

Many of us have said, "Of course I love you!" to a partner who responds, "Then why don't you act like it?" In their eyes, our behavior was not congruent with our emotions. And many of us have been shocked to find that a valued employee left our organization because he or she felt unappreciated. "I can't believe it, I always thought Katie was the best. She should have known that!" But, somehow, she did not. Our actions failed to convey how we actually felt.

While it may be difficult to ascertain what behaviors convince others that we sincerely care, the effort required to do so has its rewards. The president of a chemical manufacturing company put it this way: "Loyalty is fragile. It is built or destroyed daily. At the executive level, this means that extraordinary care must be taken to keep consideration for employees a part of every corporate decision. Only then will people enthusiastically identify with the company."

Loyalty Principle #3: People have multiple loyalties that may complement or compete with one another.

Loyalty to an employer does not have to mean disloyalty to other important parts of life. A new definition of loyalty allows for balance among multiple loyalties, including family, personal ethics and overall career goals. Properly positioned so that all loyalties enhance one another, organizational loyalty profits the individual as well as the organization.

Western Ontario University developed a strategic plan with multiple loyalties in mind. It concluded with these words: "We must also acknowledge and deal with the fact that inviting uncertainty, the risk of occasional failure, and a certain amount of dislocation demand that we respect the loyalty to self that a staff member must have. The institution cannot expect an individual to make great sacrifices at personal expense. We will not succeed unless we create an environment in which personal and institutional goals are reinforcing."

When building organizational loyalty, other deeply held concerns of the workforce must always be kept in mind. If loyalty to the company conflicts with other personally important loyalties, the employee may become stressed and unhappy, and his work is likely to suffer. Instead, management can find ways to "stack" multiple loyalties so that each one is seen as supportive of the others.

For example, it is not unusual these days to find employees with a heightened sense of loyalty to the customer. One technician I spoke with works for an aircraft manufacturer, making airplane "skin." His main loyalty is not to his company, his boss or his co-workers, but rather to the future passengers of the aircraft. He has found that this loyalty is not stacked with loyalty to his employers, since he has been reprimanded many times for demanding rigid adherence to specifications.

This worker was viewed as a troublemaker by the organization, which failed to understand that conflicting loyalties are at the root of the problem. Perhaps a different employer could have defused the situation by finding ways to wed the employee's sense of obligation to the customer with pride in workmanship and company loyalty.

Conflicting loyalties weaken organizational loyalty just as surely as complementary loyalties can strengthen it. Managers who work with the principle of multiple loyalties help subordinates build congruent sets of loyalties. One such manager told me: "I help people find out what they are loyal to, what their personal and career goals are. Then I show them how the opportunities at this organization can best support their other loyalties."

SO WHAT IF IT ISN'T FOREVER?

Today it is more effective to think of loyalty in terms of flexible "temporary systems" — much like a sport team or a movie company. Gene Hackman is an Academy Award-winning actor. Interviewed on the set of a movie he was making, Hackman had this to say about temporary systems: "There is an opportunity for intensity in work, for closeness in working relationships and for mutual commitment to a common goal. It is exciting and full."

Temporary systems by their very nature are relatively short-term liaisons between people constructed around a common purpose. These fast-paced, new systems require a strong commitment, trust and mutual expressions of loyalty for them to be successful. In the old "family" model, workers might hold onto the security of employment in exchange for a lifetime of loyalty. But this system neither nourishes nor does justice to the growth potential of organizations or of individuals in today's rapidly changing business climate. As a result, people are beginning to recognize the benefits of adopting the temporary-system outlook. At Johnson Wax, a privately held company in the Midwest, one worker said candidly: "I wish we'd stop referring to this as a family. It 's not. It's a business. We're not necessarily going to be together forever, but that doesn't mean we can't care about each other and show mutual respect."

An astronaut mission, with its need for total care, total respect and total responsibility for the team, is a good example of a temporary system working under conditions where short-term, but absolute loyalty is essential for survival.

THE NEW PARTNERSHIP

In progressive organizations across the country, a new kind of relationship grounded in mutual trust and respect is emerging between employers and employees. This new compact is developed out of realistic expectations on both sides. It is a path that reflects the new reality for business and society in a global market, as it attempts to align the interests of the organization with those of its employees, to share both the risks and rewards of doing business.

As leaner companies rely on fewer employees to shoulder more of the work, the developing relationship between company and worker is changing from paternalism to partnership: Companies owe it to their workforce to aggressively pursue new ideas, products, services, markets and customers. Employees expect to be treated fairly, to develop professionally and to have meaningful, challenging work. In return, employees owe the organization their willingness to participate in business growth, idea development, customer service and organizational transformation. Balancing the employee-employer compact is not a matter of adding more items to one side of the balance sheet or eliminating some from the other side. Increasingly, it is a matter of finding items that are of value to both the employer and the employee.

CREATING THE NEW COMPACT

Like many other companies, Royal Bank of Canada (RBC) was looking for ways to move from an entitlement-based culture to a performance-based culture. Unlike many companies, RBC took a 93-person cross-section of their workforce off site for a week-long conference to create the basis for their changing employee-employer relationship. The group drafted this outline of the new understanding to be presented to all employees: "If you buy into the organization's values and goals, contribute energy and ideas, grow and develop personally, and take care of our customers — then together we will create a good work environment, provide all the challenge you can handle, help you develop new skills and broaden your experience, and offer support and guidance for career and professional growth. And, you'll be a part of a company setting the pace in its industry; you will enjoy working here, manage the pressure, and see how the pieces fit together."

PARTNERSHIPS FOR AN EMERGING WORKPLACE

Royal Bank Group provides

- Training, learning, development opportunities
- Rewards, recognition, pay for your contribution
- Challenging job and growth opportunities
- Technology support
- Support for employability, marketability
- Support for personal and family needs
- Professional HR support

Employee provides

- Commitment to work, teamwork and customer

- Work skills in keeping with changing jobs
- Contribution focused on business objectives
- Personal ownership of development and growth
- Flexibility
- Effective people management
- Attitude

Allstate never set out to create a document about the changing employee-employer partnership. The organization had just rolled out its program on diversity education, and the diversity team was given the task of creating the next phase — how to keep renewing the organization's commitment to diversity. A team member came up with the idea of crafting a formalized statement of mutual commitments between employees and employer. And that idea initiated a process of discussions with leaders and key employees in both informal one-on-one settings and structured focus-group sessions. The document that was created as a result of this participation is:

THE ALLSTATE PARTNERSHIP

Allstate expects you to:

1. Perform at levels that significantly increase our ability to outperform the competition.
2. Take on assignments critical to meeting business objectives.
3. Continually develop needed skills.
4. Willingly listen to and act upon feedback.
5. Demonstrate a high level of commitment to achieving company goals.
6. Exhibit no bias in interactions with colleagues and customers.

7. Behave consistently with Allstate's ethical standards.

8. Take personal responsibility for each transaction with our customers and for fostering their trust.

9. Continually improve processes to address customers' needs.

You should expect Allstate to:

1. Offer work that is meaningful and challenging.

2. Promote an environment that encourages open and constructive dialogue.

3. Recognize you for your accomplishments.

4. Provide competitive pay and rewards based on your performance.

5. Advise you on your performance through regular feedback.

6. Create learning opportunities through education and job assignments.

7. Support you in defining career goals.

8. Provide you with information and resources to perform successfully.

9. Promote an environment that is inclusive and free from bias.

10. Foster dignity and respect in all interactions.

11. Establish an environment that promotes a balance of work and personal life.

———

Postscript: The former chairman of Allstate, Jerry Choate, assumed his leadership role at a time of dramatic change. Allstate was in the process of becoming a publicly held company, and in the midst of restructuring and reengineering. Choate wanted to clarify for employees that, despite change, in good times and tough times, there were certain fundamentals they could count on. He decided that committing to this partnership and putting it in writing was the most important thing he could do.

Over time, The Partnership became institutionalized. Leaders were evaluated to make sure they explained to subordinates what The Partnership meant, and employees held management accountable for behaviors that exemplified it. When Ed Liddy became chairman, he brought with him the goal of creating a high-performance culture. When asked if The Partnership was still valid, Liddy reviewed the document and decided not to change a word: "I want every employee to know that they can still count on what we've stated here. And, as I look at what we ask of employees in return ... well, to me that is the essence of high performance." So The Partnership remains a guiding force at Allstate — with both sides of the compact viewed as crucial for success.

CUSTOMIZING THE NEW COMPACT

In sales, knowing that there is no universal "sales pitch" is crucial to success, as the following story illustrates: An insurance salesman stuck his head into a sales manager's office door and said, "You probably don't want to buy any insurance, do you?"

"Young man, whoever taught you to sell? You never say, 'You don't want to buy insurance, do you?'" The sales manager continued to lecture the young man on salesmanship, stressing that every customer's needs are different. "What you lack is confidence. I'll buy some of your insurance to build your confidence."

After the appropriate papers were signed, the sales manager said, "Now remember what I told you. Every customer is different. You must use a different approach for each customer." "Oh, I do that already," said the salesman. "This is my approach for sales managers, and it works almost every time."

Forward-thinking organizations know that there is no universal approach to defining the new employer-employee relationship. Every company needs to collaborate with its workers to find the mutually beneficial arrangement appropriate to that enterprise. You can use the following as a guide for creating the new employer-employee compact in your organization:

#1. Query the workforce. At Kinsey Consulting Services, we have developed a "Loyalty/Retention Index" that measures those employee perceptions, attitudes and opinions that pertain to the ability of organizations to attract, retain and gain the commitment of talented employees. It provides the means to analyze and diagnose which elements are most critical to the loyalty and retention of your workforce, and to indicate areas in which you are most vulnerable. (For more information, please contact me by phone: 510-526-1727, email: CGoman@CKG.com, or visit my web site: www.CKG.com.)

But you don't have to bring in an outside firm. Email a questionnaire to the entire workforce and gather employees' answers to the following questions, then communicate the results to the entire organization. (An interesting and often insightful exercise is to have employees fill out the questionnaire first, then have senior managers fill it out the way they *think* employees have responded and compare the responses.)

- How do you define workplace loyalty/commitment?
- How do you show that you are loyal to your organization? (What work behaviors, attitudes and other actions demonstrate your commitment?)
- How does management already show that it is loyal or committed to you? (What policies, strategies, benefits, behaviors, attitudes, etc. demonstrate its commitment?)
- What would you specifically *want* management to do to demonstrate commitment/loyalty? (What policies, strategies, benefits, behaviors, attitudes do you want most from management?)

- Does being loyal to the organization conflict with any other of the important commitments in your life? (Does it conflict with your commitment to yourself, your family, the customer, the community, your values, etc.? And, if it does, how does it conflict?)

#2. Create a forum for discussion and interaction. Include the entire company or use a task force from a cross-section of management and employees. The purpose of the forum is to explore the kinds of employer-employee relationships that are evolving in today's leading organizations. Use the information you gathered from the questionnaires as a way to stimulate a candid discussion. Then address these specifics:

- What was the traditional workplace compact between this organization and its employees? (What did employees expect when they first joined the company? What did they think the company expected from them?)
- What part(s) of the old relationship will remain viable for the organization and its workforce in a changing business environment? (Is there any part of the "old deal" that will work in the future?)
- How are other organizations approaching this issue? (Use my examples from earlier in this chapter or from other companies that have developed a viable new compact between employers and employees.)
- What does *this* organization need most from its employees and what can it realistically offer?
- What do *our* employees want from the organization and what are they willing to give?
- Based on the new reality of a constantly changing business environment and workplace, what kind of

relationship is mutually beneficial to management and workers? (What's our "new deal?")

THE COMPACT IN ACTION

Today's workforce is scared, scarred and skeptical. They are wisely withholding their emotional investment. Before they care about their companies, they want to be sure their companies care about them.

After interviewing thousands of employees and after being involved with the "compact negotiation" process in several organizations, I find many of the same employee needs and demands coming up again and again. While your organization may be unique, the following are areas that are becoming part of what I call a "culture for commitment" in many companies:

1. Open and honest communication
2. Growth and development
3. Equity and fairness
4. Participation
5. Work-life balance
6. Recognition and appreciation

As you read through the rest of this chapter, take note of what other organizations are doing in these areas and use them as "benchmarks" for your own corporate culture.

Open and Honest Communication.

When a vice president took over a new department, she made this announcement to her staff: "I can keep you informed in either of two ways. I can let you know what is happening as soon as I know anything definite, or I can keep you informed of everything I learn — but you have to remember, some of this information will be sketchy, half-formed and sometimes not totally accurate."

Unanimously, her staff chose the second option.

Candid communication means sharing knowledge — especially important in challenging times. While some organizations find it difficult to let employees in on the details of negative decisions, Reell Manufacturing Corporation communicates candidly to employees about what they can expect from the organization during a downturn in business. When new employees join Reell they receive a guidance manual that, among other things, defines the company's philosophy of employment security. The manual states: "When short-term imbalances occur in our workplace, we could follow the example of some other companies and quickly lay people off or encourage people to leave. We do not think that is a wise choice. In the history of Reell we've never laid anyone off or let anyone go due to a short-term change in business conditions. There have been times when we've found it necessary to freeze pay or even reduce pay in order to protect our long-term future. When this happens, we all share the burden. We are committed to providing secure employment and a stable income for all regular co-workers as long as the corporation can at least break even. In the event that payroll reductions are necessary, we'll share the available work and pay rather than expect any of our regular co-workers to be deprived of employment. If conditions ever deteriorate to the point where we cannot break even, even by payroll reductions, we will seek input from all other co-workers before the triad (the senior leadership group) determines an effective response."

In the autumn of 1995, this policy was put to the test. Reell's sales forecasts for the following year were $14 million. In January, though, that projection suddenly fell to $11 million when a key customer greatly reduced its order. In line with Reell's stated philosophy, workers were first asked to reduce non-payroll expenses. The results were substantial, but not sufficient to cover the shortfall, so Reell leadership held a company-wide meeting at which employees were given a 30-day notice before implementing an across-the-board pay reduction of 10 percent. At that meeting, employees were given a complete account of the process senior management had gone through in weighing options before arriving at their decision. At the end of the meeting, the employee audience spontaneously applauded. Five months later, loyalty remained high, profits were back up again, and salaries were restored.

Why was the salary cut-back at Reell so successful? Here are the answers according to Steve Wikstrom, the current co-CEO: "We have *wired* the organization in an open and honest way. Employees didn't make the decision, but they knew how we did and *why* we did. One of the benefits of letting the workforce in on the entire process is that it exposes people to the complexity of the situation, they get to see the struggle we go through, and they really understand that there are no easy answers. We succeeded because we gave employees candid and thorough information."

There will always be times when you are not able or at liberty to discuss what you know with staff. When you don't have all the details yourself, for example, it is best to make this clear. It is also more acceptable to employees to hear that you cannot divulge rather than to be told "I don't know" when they have reason to suspect that you do.

But candor is not just for times of crisis. In order to develop trust, it is absolutely essential that subordinates know they can rely on management for honest, complete information about company matters and about personal performance appraisal. When leaders share their understanding of the organization's goals, and give candid feedback on job performance as it relates to those goals, employees develop a longer-range view of the company and their place in it.

Imagine an organization where every member is willing and able to wear many hats, communicate quickly and question the status quo with direct superiors. This is how one of the most efficient agencies in the federal government operates. The U.S. Coast

Guard encourages and supports the open flow of information. When commanding officers meet they are asked to leave their "shoulder boards" (indicative of rank) outside the room. Without the formal display of rank, subordinates feel freer to challenge ineffective policies and provoke change.

Growth and Development

There is a strong positive correlation between employees' perceptions of their future opportunities with their present employer and their commitment to that employer. If organizations are serious about building an incentive for longer-term loyalty, they need to focus on succession planning, leadership development, special assignments, job shadowing, training programs and ongoing feedback. The best employers understand the important link between development and loyalty.

This growing awareness of the importance of training to employees and employers can be seen in corporate programs across America. One example is Intel's Corporate Staffing Program — a strategic redeployment process that allows talented employees to move quickly from one business within the organization to another. This is part of Intel's new employee compact that holds workers accountable for their continued employability and holds the company accountable for informing and training workers so they will be employable. Intel informs employees about which businesses are declining and which are emerging or expanding, so that people have adequate time to plan for their redeployment. Intel utilizes information systems to provide employees with direct access to job opportunities and skill requirements, and provides them with resources to assess their existing competencies, identify knowledge gaps, hone skills, deepen training or even retrain completely.

Another example is the Workforce Development Program at USAA. USAA is a worldwide insurance and diversified financial services association headquartered in San Antonio, Texas. Many companies, when finding themselves with a workforce that no longer has the skills needed to do their jobs, simply fire those employees and hire new ones with the requisite skills. At USAA, they have made a commitment to provide re-skilling opportunities to all employees. As a direct response to the issue of worker employability, the Workforce Development Program (WDP) was created to provide employees the necessary information and resources for self-assessment, tailored education, training and skills enhancement to prepare them for current and future jobs. Going beyond a traditional approach to skills-building, the WDP helps employees understand what USAA believes it will need in five to 10 years in terms of skills and human resources, and how to improve their chances of staying employable. While career assessments and counseling have been available at USAA for many years, this new program helps focus available programs and resources. Centers throughout the company help employees to obtain information about opportunities within USAA, receive one-on-one guidance on enhancing their employability and access a wide variety of resources. The program is designed to help employees discover what they aspire to, and how those aspirations can be tailored to fit the USAA of tomorrow.

My favorite example of the importance a company puts on growth and development is the office-furniture company, Herman Miller, where performance reviews have been replaced by annual "personal planning sessions." Here is how employees are asked to prepare for these sessions:

- Please prepare a brief review … of how you feel you have done in comparison to your annual plan. What is the most important achievement in your area?
- Describe your personal plans for continuing education and development for the coming year.

- Please think about ways for us to approach our accountability (with many others) for the future of the corporation and our joint accountability for your future career in the corporation. What kind of changes will be required by the growth picture we are plotting?
- Please identify five key projects and/or goals you have as a key leader at Herman Miller and in which you feel I can be of help or support.

The Equity Factor

In many ways, American workers have grown up. They no longer believe in the idea of a paternalistic employer. Seeking greater autonomy, employees have also worked to professionalize their occupations. Many belong to associations and societies and are familiar with industry standards for treatment and pay. Today's employees are better educated and informed about their occupations, their organizations and their rights than they were even as recently as 10 years ago.

As companies downsize, restructure and refocus, employees are asked to do more and work harder. And they have, on the whole. But many feel that they have not been fairly rewarded for their increased productivity, and their resentment is most frequently seen in their reaction to executive compensation. Big disparities in pay between executives and the workforce — especially in times of downsizing and plant closures — can damage employee loyalty.

Recently I talked with an employee who was having second thoughts about her commitment to her company. "I've been with this organization for over 15 years," she told me. "I've always loved my job and felt like an important part of the company — as though we were all in this together. I've enjoyed the good times and always understood when salaries or benefits had to be reduced during the hard times. I used to be a 'gung-ho' employee. Well, last month I read that our CEO is one of the highest paid executives in the world; I also know that we just had a very profitable year. But in spite of that, we're being asked to take cuts in our health-care and other benefits. For the first time, I'm wondering if my loyalty has been misplaced." Another employee looked at how budget cuts were handled: "The biggest budget cuts were employee-focused. They eliminated all our merit increases, rewards and recognition programs — and then the top management got bonuses." The issue in both these examples wasn't just executive compensation, but also the inequity it represented.

To energize a workforce, it is going to be increasingly important that companies develop equitable relationships that reflect a true partnership. Here are some ways to address the equity factor in your organization:

1. Share the credit for success.

Be generous when handing out credit for an accomplishment. A television director who had been employed by CBS for over 25 years told me: "There are two ways you can 'pull' a performance from a cast and crew. One is to intimidate them. The other is to put your ego aside and make everyone as big a part of the overall success as possible. I've tried both ways. The second works better."

2. Share the money.

Pay may not be the most important thing, but unless employees are independently wealthy, it is still a crucial issue. So the first compensation rule is that you must offer a competitive salary/ wage for any given position. And then remember that many companies are looking at compensation that goes way beyond salary.

At Starbucks Corporation, which provides all employees — even part-time store clerks — with health insurance, stock options, training and career counseling, staff turnover is less than 60% annually, well below the 300% restaurant industry average.

SC Johnson Wax turns profit-sharing into an annual celebration. This privately held company, which has provided profit sharing to its employees since 1917, distributes an initial payment to workers in June. Then, in December, the year-end check distribution becomes a major event. All headquarters-based employees (about 3,000) are invited to attend an elaborate holiday party, business update and employee-recognition ceremony — and to receive their bonus checks. The program concludes at about noon, and that marks the official end of the workday as well as the beginning of the corporate-wide Christmas/New Year's holiday. The festivity, excitement and spirit of camaraderie end the year with exactly the kind of spirit that Johnson Wax is famous for engendering in its employees.

When looking at ways to build equity into compensation, one interesting alternative is found at Johnsonville Foods. Compensation there is spread over four pay ranges, depending on one's level of influence: Level 1 pays people who are able to manage themselves in their own jobs. (If you can't do this within the first 90 days, you can't stay at Johnsonville Foods!) At Level 2, pay increases as staff members are able to influence other members of their work group. Level 3 pays staff members more for being able to influence others throughout the entire organization. And, at Level 4, members are rewarded for being able to influence the entire industry.

Benefits are similar to pay. If other like businesses are offering certain benefits, you will have to offer them, too. The more astute businesses offer "cafeteria style" benefits, enabling employees to pick and choose which benefits are best for them.

3. Give and get objective performance appraisals.

It is crucial for employee development that they have accurate and clear feedback about their talents as well as those areas they need to improve on. It is equally important for leaders to get objective feedback from workers on what *they* do very well and not so well. Federal Express, Kraft, State Farm Insurance, TRW, Merck and Levi Strauss & Co., are just a few of the successful organizations that augment traditional management performance appraisals with 360-degree performance appraisals.

And, by the way, the days of the annual performance review are quickly becoming irrelevant. Employees want to know how well (or poorly) they are doing on the job, and they want these assessments to be fast, honest and frequent. Employees need to be involved in an ongoing dialogue about how their efforts support the organization's business strategy and what impact future changes will have on their work and careers. Most of all, they are looking for information on upcoming classes, training and job assignments that will help to expand and develop their own value.

4. Look at retention from an equitable perspective.

The relationship between employees and organizations has changed from one based on a long-term agreement to one that addresses the temporary nature of most business liaisons. Just remember that people want to work at organizations they care about — even if it's not forever — and organizations need workers who care.

As I have noted earlier, any one of a variety of forces may dictate that an individual (or a function, or an entire department) no longer serves the goals of the organization. Employees need to understand this reality and accept that there are other ways for employers to display commitment beyond a promise of ongoing employment.

A similar reality must be accepted by employers. According to current Department of Labor statistics, today's new employees will, on average, have a dozen jobs and as many as three or four different careers during their lifetimes. Workforce retention no longer equals loyalty — it is only one manifestation of loyalty. There are many forces (lifestyle choices, family obligations, personal development, etc.) that may influence a loyal employee to leave an organization. Sue Swenson, the president of Leap Wireless, tells employees that she expects them to leave the company if they are offered a better opportunity elsewhere.

5. Don't ask others to do anything you wouldn't do yourself.

When the Chevron plant in Richmond, California, needed to mandate arbitrary drug testing for employees, all senior managers submitted to the testing for a full year before asking employees to do likewise. Leading by example takes a willingness to observe the same set of standards and performance criteria that you require from others.

6. Increase sensitivity to areas that might be perceived as inequitable.

A close look at the psychology of relationships reveals that most individuals automatically attempt to keep a mental balance between what they contribute to a relationship and what they get back from it. When employees believe that they are putting more into their company than they are getting back, or when they do not perceive the rewards distribution to be equitable, commitment slips dramatically. As employees look for balance through equitable treatment, it is their *perception* of the treatment, rather than the treatment itself that defines reality.

I interviewed employees at a public utility where workers were negotiating a two-percent raise that management was resisting. At that same time, the fleet of corporate vans was repainted. Instead of viewing this as a necessary expense, the employees' perception was that it was unfair of the company to spend money on vehicles while it argued about a salary increase with employees: "How dare they throw money at those trucks and then quibble about a lousy two-percent raise!"

The retired CEO of a chemical manufacturing company put it this way: "Commitment is built or destroyed every day. As a leader you must make it a routine part of your decision-making process to ask the question: Will this action be *perceived* as equitable?"

7. Value diversity.

Valuing differences — having an appreciation of what makes people unique — is not only an important issue for employees, it is critical to any business needing to serve a demanding customer base in a global marketplace. Organizations that make a commitment to diversity demonstrate that commitment by their efforts to attract diverse job candidates, offer diversity education, create minority networks and celebrate diverse holidays. But the best companies don't stop there. They go beyond tolerating differences and work to build a culture that respects diversity as the fuel for creative energy and insight.

Headquartered in San Francisco, Just Desserts is a wholesale and retail baker with $14 million gross revenue. The company has been named "best bakery" by Bay Area publications for the past 30 years. Its employees include immigrants from all nationalities, gay couples, and former felons. At Just Desserts, everyone's beliefs and values are accepted and people are encouraged to be themselves. Employees are evaluated on two things: doing their job and getting along with fellow workers. "You can't find the best, most creative solutions unless people are free to be who they are," says the CEO, Elliott Hoffman. "If employees are uncomfortable, anxious, or angry, they shut down and don't do their best work."

The desire to create an inclusive environment, where everyone feels valued and where everyone is able to contribute, is quickly permeating the most successful organizations in America. The following is excerpted from a letter to Marriott managers from the Lodging Director of Diversity: "Each Marriott manager will play a leadership role in making diversity a part of our corporate culture. This will require us to look beyond mere compliance with the law; we must begin to see diversity as an *asset to our business* and *encourage the special talents and diverse perspectives* of each associate to produce quality service of superior value for all of our customers. Diversity should not be referred to as a fad, project or program, because *diversity is a long-term commitment to organizational change.*"

Employee Participation

As important as honest communication from above is, today's talented employees want more: They are looking for a dialogue, not a monologue. Many of America's best leaders build employee loyalty by turning communication into a conversation. One such CEO told me: "We communicate with our people like crazy. Quarterly our employees tell us what to do."

Empowerment, employee involvement, participation and broadening individual responsibility are all ways to describe a workplace trend that gives employees control over decisions affecting them. Employees today are seeking more freedom of choice and more authority. Companies that empower employees in this way are already reaping the benefits.

At Ritz-Carlton, employees are empowered as teams to solve problems that directly affect them. Here's how it works: if a particular hotel has, as its primary customer complaint, a problem with room service taking too long, the manager would inform employees in that department and ask for volunteers to form a committee to find the root of the problem in the room service system and to change or create a different process that solves the problem. By the same token, if two different departments have a conflict — say waiters are dissatisfied with dishwashers because the banquet service isn't ready on time — then members of both departments form a cross-functional team (as internal customer and supplier) to find the process problem and solve it. According to former president

Horst Schulze, "Employees are finding the cause of the defect and eliminating it rather than correcting it temporarily." In addition to this approach to teamwork, individuals on the staff are empowered to make decisions to please or appease a customer — even when it costs the company up to $2,000 — without having to check with any supervisor.

When Lura Powell was director of Pacific Northwest National Laboratory, she found inclusion to be a powerful motivator. "If you have a central theme, values and vision — and if the staff as a whole feel they are part of it — it becomes a tremendous force. Then, people want to move forward with the company. They want to be a part of success. One of the reasons I took the job at PNNL was the opportunity to take early-stage science and technology and help it move toward commercial products. Even some of our most fundamental scientists bought into this strategy because they wanted to see their discoveries used. But, again, they felt they were part of that decision. And with inclusion, comes commitment and engagement. Then you've really got something!"

Participation is not just a "nice" thing to do for employees, it is a sound business strategy. Here's how one senior executive put it: "Our workforce will run through walls for you, if they perceive that we're all in it together. Participation unleashes behaviors and passions that I think leaders sometimes miss by trying to look strong and omnipotent — as if that is what a leader is all about. It isn't. It's not about having all the answers. It's about being open to other people contributing, providing their insights and offering diverse perspectives so that you get to the best decision, not just the leader's decision."

Work-Life Balance

Call it work-life blend, call it a need for balance — call it anything you like, but realize that this trend is one that not only won't go away, it will become even more crucial in the future to the retention of top performers. Talented employees demand more control of their time — whether it involves organizationally structured arrangements such as flex-time, flex-place, part-time or contractual work, or a corporate culture that stresses results over "face time." Companies that don't respond to this growing need will lose a competitive edge in retention and motivation. So ask people about their scheduling conflicts, and then involve them in co-creating timetables and deadlines.

At a recent business meeting on the East Coast, I met an executive who handed me his card as an introduction. I was startled when he abruptly snatched it back. He explained that he wanted to cross out the word *senior* in front of his vice-president title. He went on to tell me that he was only temporarily acting in the senior position and that, as soon as possible, he wanted to return to his old job. He said that five years earlier his ambition had been the presidency of the company, but not anymore: "Being a vice president suits me just fine. I'm good at it, and I could do it in my sleep. I don't need the added pressure of a higher position. Besides, I've got a family and a couple of interesting hobbies. This gives me time to 'play' with them."

Increasingly, people are looking to balance a variety of interests and commitments. They are not as likely to think, as do some of their bosses, that the world begins and ends with the office or factory. I've heard this sentiment expressed in a variety of ways:

"I love my job, but it's not my whole life."

"If the company ever relocated, I wouldn't move. I like my lifestyle here too much."

"My parents weren't there for me when I was growing up. I will never let a job get between me and my family."

Blending career and family life first came to corporate attention with the influx of female employees after about 1980. Then companies began to find that so-called "female" issues actually jumped gender lines: Because more women were joining DuPont's ranks, the company's affirmative action committee decided to survey employees about their child-care needs. They found that child care was not just a women's issue; it was a mainstream employment issue affecting both men and women. Those findings had significant implications for DuPont's ability to retain good staff; a subsequent study found that half of the women and a quarter of the men working at the company had considered moving to a company that offered more job flexibility.

Based on these survey findings, DuPont executives began a process of developing "work-life programs" to help employees deal with issues such as child care and elder care and to balance the demands of work and home. Fifteen years later, a survey of employees found that 52% of those who had taken advantage of the programs said they would "go the extra mile" for DuPont, compared to 36% of those who had not used the programs.

Other organizations are expanding their efforts to help employees balance the work-life seesaw. Last year I worked with a company that centered its reengineering efforts around the key question: *What gets in the way of your doing a good job and having a life?*

At the heart of all these programs and policies is a basic philosophy that takes into consideration the importance of employees' lives beyond the workplace. But no leader articulates this philosophy better or more concisely than Bob Wahlstedt, one of the cofounders of Reell Precision Manufacturing: "If there is a conflict between the job and the family, we expect the employee to resolve the matter in favor of the family."

Recognition and Appreciation

Today it's not good enough simply to command the behavior you want from employees — you've got to find a way to tap into their hearts and minds, and to elicit their best efforts. You have to make employees feel valued so they all want to do their best work on a daily basis, to consistently act in the best interests of the organization. And for people to want to give their all, they have to feel valued, included and appreciated.

When employees today speak of recognition and appreciation, they're talking about an ongoing acknowledgement of their contribution to the organization. Workers are looking for respect, trust and personal attention. Organizations validate these needs when they:

1. Make sure that all appreciation is genuine and heartfelt.

If you don't mean it, don't do it. Gone are the days when an annual "gesture" of recognition — the company picnic or awards dinner — can compensate for callous treatment by management during the rest of the year. One unhappy employee put it this way: "How stupid do they think we are? Do they really believe that a lousy chicken dinner is going to make up for treating us like robots?"

And, whatever else you do, keep your sense of humor. Leaders at all levels endear themselves to employees when they help people "lighten up" and have fun while they work. Sometimes the rewards that make the most lasting impressions are the small, "silly" things — the bouquet of balloons, the funny thank-you card, the singing telegram or the award "roast."

2. Include spontaneous recognition.

Don't make all rewards so predictable or systematic that they become a version of "if it's Tuesday, it must be Recognition Day." Nothing loses meaning faster than the scramble to designate an "employee of the month" *every* month. In contrast to recognition programs that are stilted by their predictability, spontaneous, on-the-spot awards immediately acknowledge positive behaviors.

Recognition is the most meaningful when it is given as soon as possible after the desired behavior or performance, and many leading companies are using some form of spontaneous recognition: The Bravo Zulu (Navy talk for "well done") program at Federal Express gives managers the prerogative of awarding a dinner, theater tickets or cash to any employee who is "caught" doing an outstanding job. And Wells Fargo Bank gave this concept an innovative twist when 16,000 employees were each given awards of $35 to present to a co-worker. This peer-to-peer recognition had two distinct advantages: First, the employees knew better than their bosses who actually deserved a special acknowledgement, and second, for each $35 spent, two people felt great!

3. Give people personalized recognition.

Do unto others as they would have you do unto them. As leaders respond to the changing needs and perceptions of subordinates and staff, more companies are dumping old-fashioned award certificates and are bestowing career-boosting privileges upon their best workers, such as a chance to increase their visibility, responsibility or authority. Examples of such opportunities can include time with the boss over dinner or lunch, trips to other locations for special training, meeting important customers, participating in strategic planning sessions, making presentations to senior management or representing the company at professional gatherings. And remember — one of the most meaningful recognition "strategies" is still a simple and sincere "thank you," given one-on-one from boss to employee.

Employees are individuals who are motivated in different ways. By staying sensitive to people's uniqueness, leaders can tailor recognition to recipients. A boss I know acknowledged the extra time and effort put in by her team with one set of letters of gratitude sent to the employees and another to their families. Sending personal letters to employees' homes might not be appropriate in all cases, but in this situation the leader knew her staff well and she understood the difficulties that the overtime demands had created for their families. The result was that her team felt doubly rewarded.

At another company, the boss has each member of his staff fill out a personal profile of hobbies, favorite sports and preferences for leisure activities. Then, when he wants to reward a staff member, he goes through the employee's profile and produces tickets for the ballet, a round of golf, dinner out, etc. — whatever reflects the employee's personal interests.

Kirk Malcki, president of Pegasus Personal Fitness Centers in Dallas, asks new physical-fitness trainers to make a list of rewards, ranging in value from $25 to $200, they would like to receive for reaching weekly and monthly goals. Instead of commonplace prizes, his 15 employees have opted for tickets to rock-concerts, limousine rentals and half-days off. Thanks in part to the more personalized incentives, sales have more than doubled in six years.

4. Treat people with courtesy and respect.

A most critical element is respect. To what depth do your employees feel that you respect and sincerely care about them as individuals? Respecting an employee means that his/her opinions count, that appreciation and recognition are shown for good work and that the employee feels listened to. Gallup research has found that peak performers in a variety of organizations feel that someone at work cares about them and their personal progress. They report that someone regularly and frequently asks about their progress.

Trust, respect and consistency in relationships have always been important to business success. These traits, however, take on added significance today. To show your appreciation for their contribution to the organization, give people your full attention: listen to them, *hear* them, encourage their questions, support their ambitions and respond to their ideas with careful consideration. Walt Blankley, the former CEO of AMETEK, put it this way: "A leader is first of all a communicator. But one of the most important parts of communication is listening. And you must really listen, not just use techniques, like repeating what the person has just said, so that you *appear* to listen. I mean displaying genuine respect. I talk with people on the shop floor, and they're too smart to be taken in by some phony technique. They know if it's real."

5. Show people how their efforts make a difference.

Corporate leaders must set the loyalty agenda, articulating how an employee's participation contributes to the greater good of the organization. That greater good must involve doing something more than contributing to the bottom line and building market share. It ultimately has to do with values, mission, purpose and being connected to something greater than themselves.

Most people want to do more than just bring home a paycheck; they want to *believe in* their work. They want to contribute in meaningful ways, and then they want to see how their contributions make a difference. When Ford Motor Company created the Taurus automobile, they took a prototype on tour to the various parts suppliers. By doing this, they showed exactly how those suppliers' products contributed to the value of the finished product. The response was overwhelming. Employees from each company wrote unsolicited letters pledging to continue their best efforts on behalf of Ford.

Steve Wikstrom, co-CEO at Reell, talked to me about how leaders can miss a chance to build motivation by being too efficient: "People want to know that they are significant, and that what they do matters. They want the experience of belonging and being appreciated for their contributions. As a leader, this is an area where you must be careful *not* to be so efficient that you become ineffective. If I have 200 employees, it is useless to try showing appreciation to every one of them every week — even though that strategy looks highly efficient. But it can make a tremendous difference in their motivation if I spend several minutes with a half-dozen workers during the week, showing my appreciation for the job they are doing and reinforcing how that job fits into the bigger picture."

6. Increase challenge and autonomy

Employees who feel good about their jobs are more loyal. A job that involves a high degree of autonomy will increase motivation and satisfy needs for growth and achievement.

Restructuring jobs so that they offer more autonomy and challenge is a step managers can easily take to increase job satisfaction. And when work is more challenging and interesting, people will work more attentively and constructively. I spoke with secretaries on an exciting task force who found themselves eagerly taking home piles of paper for the first time in their careers. I spoke with front-line employees who devoted Saturdays to a special project because they were "fascinated with the work."

THE HIGH COST OF LOST LOYALTY

Lost loyalty is expensive. It is estimated to cost American business $60 billion annually. It has been linked to high absenteeism, low productivity, poor quality and increased employee theft. To appreciate the lost loyalty price your organization may be paying, estimate the expense you incur when replacing a valuable employee: hiring, training, relocation costs, as well as the price paid in decreased production and quality while the new employee gets up to speed.

Some expenses are more difficult to quantify. What is the possible cost to your corporate reputation when disloyal employees "bad mouth" the organization to family, friends or co-professionals? How might this affect other workers, potential employees, current and potential customers? How vulnerable are you to employee sabotage? The existence of computer viruses increases the damage that can be done by disloyal individuals. A *Fortune* magazine article entitled "The Trust Gap" reported increased cases of employee sabotage by workers who felt they had been unfairly treated and therefore lost all loyalty to their organizations. In one example, an oil company employee erased a database worth millions of dollars, causing all drilling and exploration to be suspended worldwide until the file could be recreated.

Finally, how can you calculate the financial impact of talented employees who no longer care about the company — who report to work physically but not emotionally, who hold back creative suggestions, who reduce the effort they are willing to expend on the job?

THE BENEFITS OF EMPLOYEE LOYALTY TO THE ORGANIZATION

Organizations need employee loyalty; that is, they need the caring and emotional attachment of dedicated workers. When employees are committed to their work and to the goals of the organization, employers can expect to see that their organizations will:

- Attract talented employees
- Increase employee retention
- Increase customer loyalty
- Increase employee motivation
- Increase corporate profitability
- Increase employee willingness to put out extra effort

Attract talented people

Loyalty is tied directly to the health and quality of the corporate culture. Organizations that treat people well, placing emphasis on future development and providing opportunities for growth, generate allegiance and commitment. Even at a time when jobs are scarce, employers need to recognize that if they have not worked to maintain employee commitment, they will experience a dramatic problem with employee retention as the economy improves. Employers, managers and supervisors who take steps to win their employees' loyalty now will reap the benefits of attracting the top talent.

Increase Employee Retention

The new social compact is short-term. Employees now carry their skills with them from one company to another, and many workers consider job-hopping a normal route to professional success. Ultimately, of course, it is the best professionals who have most options to go elsewhere and give their ideas and commitment to other organizations.

Companies have always understood that customers are volunteers. They need to understand that, increasingly, employees are volunteers, too. Talented workers have options. If an organization wants to become the employer of choice for the best and brightest, it must develop the kind of work environment that retains good people.

Increase Customer Loyalty

In one way or another, we are all in the service business; we rely on customer loyalty for profits, not just for market share. Research at Harvard Business School estimates that a five-percent increase in customer loyalty can produce profit increases of between 25 and 85 percent. Loyalty is a direct result of consistent customer satisfaction. Customer satisfaction is a direct result of the treatment received in those "moments of truth" every time customers interact with employees. And remember, the relationship between the employee and customer is almost always a reflection of the relationship between the employee and the organization. Maintaining customer loyalty is impossible without loyal employees who are committed to the service goals of the organization, and who are willing to extend their best efforts to ensure that customers come back time and time again.

Increase Profits

A company's ability to foster employee morale and loyalty is attracting rapidly growing scrutiny along Wall Street. Ernst & Young's Center for Business Innovation presented a study to The Council of Institutional Investors showing that investor decisions are 35-percent driven by non-financial factors. One "people factor," a company's ability to attract and retain talented employees, ranks fifth among the 39 factors that investors use in picking stocks — right behind strategy execution, management credibility, quality of strategy and innovation.

It is enlightening to apply this concept to personal experience. Recall a time when you were working for an organization to which you had tremendous loyalty. Compare that to another work experience in which your loyalty was minimal. Answer these simple questions:

- How specifically did the first company profit from your high loyalty?
- What were the costs of your lower loyalty to the second company?

Increase Employee Willingness to Put Out Extra Effort

In our post-Industrial world it is not capital assets that will determine the success of an organization, but rather the willingness of its employees to change and improve in order to meet or set the next standard of excellence. Employees who are emotionally involved with the organization are far more productive than those who have emotionally withdrawn. Companies need employees who are enlightened and willing to participate in a vital, competitive business environment. When I ask employees how they show commitment and loyalty, the response I hear most often is that they are willing to increase their efforts — to "go the extra mile."

Even when it is difficult to put a price on it, leaders know intuitively that employee commitment is immensely valuable. The president of a high-tech company in Silicon Valley summed up the opinions of many leaders I've interviewed: "If given the choice between working with a group of people who are highly skilled but have low loyalty, and one of average skills and high loyalty — I'd pick the loyal group because I know that somehow they'd make it happen."

WHAT THE WORKFORCE GAINS

In my research the motivation for loyalty fell into three distinct categories:

Transactional: "I give because I get." Some employees are loyal because in their organizations loyalty is acknowledged, rewarded, and reciprocated.

Inspirational: "I'm attracted to the organization because of what it stands for." Other employees are inspired to loyalty by the specific missions, philosophies, or values of their organizations.

Integral: "That's just the way I am." The largest number of people responded that they want to be loyal because it is an integral part of who they are and how they like to approach their jobs. People were raised to be loyal: to root for local sports teams, take care of family members, wear school colors, and pledge allegiance to their country. Loyalty has powerful roots in both our highest instincts and deepest beliefs.

In an environment of mutual commitment, employees gain honest communication from management, challenging and empowering work responsibilities, recognition and appreciation for their efforts, personal/professional development opportunities, respect and equitable treatment. In addition to these tangible benefits, employees are inspired to invest emotionally in enterprises where they can commit to the goals and identify with the values of the organization.

Above all, though, employees seek to enjoy a quality of work life that includes personal satisfactions. We all want to love our work and bond emotionally with our organizations because doing so satisfies a powerful, and basic, human need to *connect with* and *contribute* to something significant. "The life committed to nothing larger than itself is a meager life indeed," writes Martin Seligman in his book *Learned Optimism.* "Human beings require a context of meaning and hope." Loyalty for most people is an inherent part of their personal work ethic. It makes work more enjoyable and fulfilling. It gives jobs meaning.

I was reminded of how deeper meaning is being sought at work when I was attending a conference last year. The speaker told the audience that we are not human beings having a spiritual experience, but rather spiritual beings having a human experience. This is a message that has been expressed often before by religious leaders and philosophers. The difference here was the audience. Our speaker was addressing 2,000 real estate employees at a national sales meeting. Peter Senge of MIT's Sloan School sums it up this way: "A corporation can't save your soul, but it can stand in for the age-old idea of people collectively pursuing a path that has real meaning to them."

The strong desire of employees to care about their organizations was something that my research found again and again. In the thousands of interviews I've conducted, I have never heard a single worker declare: "My career goal is to do mediocre work at a company I hate." Commitment and loyalty are part of what we are as human beings and how we want to relate to our work. Here is a small sample of employee comments from my interviews:

"I've always had to work where I could be loyal to the company."

"Given the choice between a higher salary and a job I loved, I'd choose the job."

"Commitment and relationship is all there is."

"The difference between a job and a 'calling' is the passion I feel about the work and the emotional attachment I have to the organization."

MANAGING FOR COMMITMENT

People increase their loyalty when they feel in partnership with their bosses. To facilitate this kind of bonding, managers must remain aware that their role has changed from one of "order-giver" to one of coach, champion and consensus-builder. Bosses who excel at coaching and delegating give employees control over their activities and agendas. As one such manager said to me: "I've finally learned to get out of people's way and off their backs."

People want to be involved at work, but they are uncertain if they can commit and trust.

People want to contribute their creative efforts, but they don't know if it's safe to take the risk.

People want to be loyal, but they don't want their loyalty to go unreciprocated.

People want visionary, trustworthy leaders who will explain the new realities and inspire commitment to the organization's success. Even when loyalty is not part of the corporate policy, individual leaders can develop high loyalty in their own teams. Leaders develop loyal employees by being loyal in return:

"My people always come first."

"You get loyalty by giving it."

"If I go all out for them, they will go all out for the company."

One vice president told an employee that she would back him to the end. If he chose to resign over an unfair company policy (as he'd threatened to do) she'd resign with him. "I meant what I said, but he changed his mind. The employee didn't want *me* to jeopardize *my* career, so he dropped the whole issue."

As a final check on your ability to engage the commitment of others, ask yourself what you expect. The powerful influence of one person's expectation on another's behavior is known as the Pygmalion Effect. Eliza Doolittle explains it in George Bernard Shaw's play *Pygmalion:* "You see, really and truly, apart from the things anyone can pick up, the difference between a lady and a flower girl is not how she behaves but how she's treated. I shall always be a flower girl to Professor Higgins because he always treats me as a flower girl and always will; but I know I can be a lady to you because you always treat me as a lady and always will."

The difference between leaders who "just can't find good people today" and those who speak with pride of the hard work and dedication of their employees may be a direct result of their attitudes toward their people.

Over the past several years, I have been a guest on many radio call-in programs. I especially remember one in the Northwest, when an unusual number of disgruntled employees were phoning in with corporate "horror stories." People complained about being unappreciated, underpaid, misunderstood. They spoke of callous treatment from uncaring bosses, and reported that they worked for organizations "just interested in making a buck." For the entire hour, calls followed the same line. Finally, in genuine disgust, the interviewer said to me: "The principles you're giving us sound so simple, why aren't more companies following them?"

I didn't have to think about my reply: "With all the diet books on the market, why aren't we all thin and trim? What could be simpler than reducing calories and increasing exercise?" The answer to my question and his is the same. Things that are simple are not necessarily easy.

As a consultant and speaker, I have worked with executives and managers around the world, and not once have I encountered a boss who despised all employees. On the contrary, the leaders I've met are good and concerned people. And even if an employer's only goal were to increase profits, the evidence is still conclusive that the best way to do it is to build commitment by attending to the well-being of talented employees.

What could be simpler? And what could be more difficult to accomplish?

What amazes me sometimes, is that so many of you do it so well.

7

LIBERATING POTENTIAL THROUGH COLLABORATION

"This isn't the company I joined. It's better!"

"I believe that folding the spirit of rugged individualism into a collaborative environment is the recipe for a successful company. People are encouraged to do their best, every day, and to apply that personal best to the good of the group. It's a demanding strategy for a company's leaders. They must believe, fiercely, that every person in the company wants to and is capable of doing great things. They must consistently and publicly reward teamwork. And they must reinforce, through their own behavior, the value of working together to accomplish a company goal, even at the occasional sacrifice of personal ego."

Lynn Casey, Chairman and Chief Executive Officer, Padilla Speer Beardsley, Inc.

"POWERS OR RESOURCES not yet developed" is the dictionary definition of potential. Applied to physics, it means latent energy waiting to be used. Applied to a workforce, it means untapped talents, ideas and contributive strengths waiting to be switched on. "No company," I always emphasize at the end of my programs, "uses more than a fraction of its workforce's total potential. The companies that do best today are the ones that find means to use a larger fraction than their competitors. That is their edge in the new global economy."

But how do they *get* that edge? is the question my audiences always ask.

By taking action, I tell them, based on two fundamental principles:

1. Rely on human potential as central to your corporate strategy.

2. Liberate that potential through creative collaboration.

A company's competitiveness is a combination of the potential of its people, the quality of the information that people possess, and a willingness to share knowledge with others in the organization. The leadership challenge is to link these components as tightly as possible. How you get the process going is up to you. No two companies are alike. No two workforces are temperamentally the same. All I can do is assure you that there is a lot of untapped potential in your workforce waiting to be liberated, and knowledge waiting to be shared. To prove it, I'll tell you some success stories about how companies are using creative collaboration to tap into that potential. Because, when it comes to sharing knowledge, building collaboration and liberating human potential, few strategies have proved more effective than the finding and telling of the right stories…

THE J.D. STEERING AXLE COMPANY:
How Jeff Garbin helped to sharpen the competitive edge at John Deere by bringing 15 people closer together.

The problem at Deere was declining cost-efficiency resulting from too much non-value-added activity in the manufacturing process, so Deere's leadership adopted the principles of "lean manufacturing" and came up with a new idea about factory floor organization.

As part of that restructuring, Deere asked Jeff Garbin to introduce the change-over in one of their departments. It was Garbin's first assignment, and the first thing he did when he became the module leader (shop supervisor) of Department 947 of the John Deere Harvester Works was to ask his 15 employees to invent a name for themselves. Thus, the Steering Axle Company was born with its corporate slogan, "A quality product built by quality people."

Deere's idea was to abandon the long-standing "cell concept" of manufacturing in which employees merely performed one or two operations on a component before passing it on to the next cell, and create instead a "modular production system" in which all employees working on a given component would share equal responsibility for the finished product. Once up and running, the newly formed modules would be treated as independent, in-house mini-companies — with their own corporate philosophies and standards — whose "business" it was to supply John Deere with top-grade, competitively priced parts for assembly into the machines and equipment it sold to the public.

Along with the other new module leaders, it was Jeff Garbin's job to help his employees through the transition. And, as "CEO" of the newly formed Steering Axle Company, he set as his own first goal "the creation of an environment where people have a mutual sense of responsibility for producing defect-free parts." Eighteen months later, these were the results: a 55-percent reduction in inventory, a material reduction of 7 percent, a direct labor reduction of 12 percent, an overhead reduction of 22 percent, and a lead time reduction of a whopping 80 percent — from 15 to 3 days. "The key to our success," Garbin explained, "was that workers took ownership and took pride and satisfaction in their jobs. My role was to facilitate that transition through empowerment backed by training and support."

Thanks to Garbin and the other "CEOs" at John Deere, the module system of manufacturing and assembly has now become the standard factory-floor model throughout the Harvester Works, and soon all of Deere's plants will be organized in the same way — a collection of autonomous, self-managed mini-companies, each wholly responsible for the quality and saleability of the component part it produces.

How did Garbin make this model work so well in the beginning? First, by eliminating "human barriers" in the collaborative process that were creating divisiveness among his workers. "We had 10 people working the early shift and five on the late shift. There were people on the two shifts who had never spoken to one another before. They didn't know each other, they came from different manufacturing disciplines and they had a reputation for not getting along. I began by getting both shifts together in a room for a couple of hours, with no limits on what they were to discuss, except that it *couldn't* be business-related. Within three months, people started coming in early or staying late just so that they could talk with people on the other shift about what was happening at work." The other thing Garbin did, as part of Deere's plan, was to bring his employees physically closer together so that each worker, whatever his task on the steering axle, was doing his job within inhaling distance of his business partners. The different tasks were still carried out individually, as in the cell system, but instead of being scattered all over the factory floor the cells were now pulled together into a single organic whole that could exchange information and share ideas whenever the need arose. As one welder put it, "My customer is about 15 feet away from me. If there's a problem we work it out right then and there. Before, I made these parts and then they went to another corner of the plant. I didn't even know the guys that took them on from me. We should have done this 20 years ago."

In the end, the collaborative obstacle Jeff Garbin had eliminated was much more basic than factory-floor inefficiency or employee indifference to John Deere's costing problems. He had eliminated isolation. Through module 947 he had turned 15 strangers into a group of friends and business associates who proved more than able to make *their* new mini-company a resounding success.

LESSONS:

- Look closely at how your workers are relating to one another personally. Don't tolerate divisiveness, resentment, disrespect, blaming, grudge-holding or mutual suspicion among departments or individuals. Creative collaboration cannot take place in an atmosphere of animosity. Get your people together however you can. It doesn't have to be work-related. Form a stock-market investment club, or a poetry society, or a softball team, or a bird-watching group — anything that will let your people know one another better as individuals. And don't hold back because you think you're intruding. How your workers get along is your business.

- When any major structural change is undertaken, the employees affected will join in the process much more enthusiastically if they understand clearly why the change is necessary and what it is meant to accomplish. Don't be mysterious. Give your workers the details, encourage feedback, take action based on constructive suggestions — and don't assume you know more than they do just because you're the boss. Probably the most compelling lesson learned from the John Deere experience was voiced by that welder: "We should have done this 20 years ago."

- Forming independent mini-companies may not solve *your* organization's problems or suit its structures, but there will always be other ways to create closer cooperation and greater responsibility in the front-line workforce. Identify the obstacles first, then plan how best to remove them, then let the workers discuss your plan among themselves and come back to you with their own ideas. I've said this before, but it's worth repeating here: A more empowered workforce is a more contributive workforce.

INTERNATIONAL COLLABORATION:
How Lockheed Martin, Northrop Grumman and
BAE Systems are creating the F-35.

The F-35 Joint Strike Fighter represents a new kind of program for Lockheed Martin. It is the largest aerospace defense contract in history and an example of a complex organization built on collaborative teams and relationships. The companies building the planes as "partners" are Lockheed Martin, Northrop Grumman and BAE Systems. The F-35 will be customized for five military services — the U.S. Navy, Air Force and Marine Corps, and the United Kingdom's Royal Air Force and Royal Navy. Other international partners involved in the F-35 JSF's development are Italy, the Netherlands, Turkey, Canada, Denmark, Norway and Australia. More than 2,500 aircraft are planned for the U.S. and the U.K., with up to 3,000 additional export sales projected.

Tom Burbage, F-35 JSF program director, likens the F-35 organizational chart to a jigsaw puzzle, with many interdependent, sometimes conflicting or competing partnerships. The vision of collaboration among competitors was born on a rationale of selecting the "best athletes." People are chosen to lead Integrated Product teams regardless of whether they are employed by the prime contractor or by a partner. And "best practices" are derived from lessons learned across all partner companies.

The challenge of international collaboration is faced every day on F-35, even at program headquarters in Fort Worth, Texas. One example was on the wing team where two managers, one from Lockheed Martin Aeronautics Co. and one from BAE Systems, had to design a system for knowledge transfer and joint learning to prepare their teams for using a new precision milling machine.

A year previously, lead manufacturing engineers from all product teams met at BAE in England to review all the tests for a new milling machine made in Germany. This machine provided high-precision machining for the inside of the wing's external skins and the surfaces of the understructure. The engineers realized that they could not test the machine's design, tooling and machining processes at any other site than BAE Systems because the machines on order would not be available in the U.S. until October 2003. The F-35 JSF program is deadline-sensitive, and managers could not afford to wait until late 2003 for their manufacturing experts to familiarize themselves with the machine tools' operation.

So, for the past six months, teams of manufacturing engineers have been traveling to BAE from Lockheed Martin plants in Fort Worth and Palmdale, Calif., and from Northrop Grumman in El Segundo, Calif., to test the new machine. A dedicated operations site was set up in England to support this testing where BAE is training the other partners. By October, when machines are delivered to the various JSF sites, the Airframe team in Fort Worth will be ready to "hit the ground running."

"It's a real learning transfer," says Andy Gillet, BAE Systems' senior manufacturing engineer on the F-35 Airframe, who is stationed in Fort Worth with his Lockheed Martin and Northrop Grumman colleagues. "When you've got a bunch of engineers together regardless of culture or country background, you give them a job to do, and they just get on with it."

His "partner" manager, Grady White, the lead manufacturing engineer on the Airframe/Wing for the project, says: "The focus on JSF is, 'Look — we are in this together, and we are going to succeed together, or we are going to fail together,' so we better do everything we can to help each other succeed. That's the motivation —

and I've seen it and I've heard it verbalized by top management. I think having a clearly defined goal and purpose helps keep us focused on this program and is a key to our success."

White continues, "My partnership with Andy Gillet is significant. We basically manage this part of the project. I don't think it would work without having him here. He really is the power to get things done back at BAE. You need someone to knock down walls to get logistics taken care of, and he has really done a great job with that. Andy and I knew each other previously in the program's Concept Demonstration phase, so we've worked together for quite awhile. That helps."

Gillet adds, "I think you've got to be more open and honest in collaboration. Just treat people the way you want to be treated yourself. It's like any partnership — with your wife, your kids, your parents, your siblings, your friends. It is just the same with the people that you work with. It's pretty simple, really."

LESSONS:

- Knowledge is transferred through people and relationships. When asked for a short definition of knowledge management, KM expert Larry Prusak stated: "Hire smart people. Let them talk."
- Social networks, those ties among individuals that are based on mutual trust, shared work experiences and common physical and virtual spaces, are at the heart of successful collaboration. Anything you can do to strengthen those ties will enhance the knowledge flow within your team or throughout your organization.

KNOWLEDGE MANAGEMENT IN ACTION:
How Fluor is building a workforce for the future.

A project manager for a natural gas project in South Africa had a question about the next step in his project — he had some doubts about specifications given by the vendor on a piece of equipment, and did not want to proceed without being sure. The issue was a showstopper. He didn't know the answer, and had to resolve the concern urgently in order to proceed with his work. Before he left the office for the day, he posted an urgent question to the knowledge community for help. By the time he got to work the following morning, he had four replies from around the world: an expert from California, another expert in Calgary, and two specialists in Vancouver. The responses confirmed that with a slight modification, his project could proceed.

This type of project problem solving occurs every day at Fluor Corporation. "This is not the first time I have had to resort to using the discussion forums to solve a problem," said the project manager. "I have found our knowledge management tool and processes indispensable and I am very encouraged by the enthusiasm of the Fluor employees who are always willing to assist. When I first heard about knowledge management, I had my doubts whether it would work. Today I have my doubts whether I could work without it."

Fluor Corporation is one of the world's largest publicly owned engineering, procurement, construction and maintenance (EPCM) service organizations. Fluor serves customers in a wide variety of traditional and evolving industries worldwide including chemicals and petrochemicals, commercial and institutional, government projects, life sciences, manufacturing, microelectronics, mining, oil and gas, power, telecommunications and transportation infrastructure. With projects all over the globe — many in remote locations — sharing knowledge on a global basis is essential to Fluor's success.

Fluor, like most corporations, is faced with a big "double whammy" challenge: an aging workforce and a growing number of jobs being work-shared overseas. Both require ways to collect knowledge — and share it before it walks out the door. Since employees are the core of Fluor's intellectual assets and the knowledge-based services strategy, their buy-in and participation are critical. How did Fluor demonstrate the value to employees while experiencing this flux in global employment? By communicating the benefit to employees — if they leverage knowledge management, they make themselves more valuable to the corporation. In addition, the following components were used as beacons illuminating the goal of becoming the world's premier knowledge-based EPCM services company:

Provide a work environment to attract, retain, develop and motivate top quality, knowledgeable, experienced employees.

Identify, nurture and apply the collective employee knowledge and expertise required to achieve business and strategic goals, enabling future growth through competitive differentiation.

Leverage knowledge from global sources to produce and apply rapid innovations anywhere in the world.

Improve the company's flexibility in shifting resources (including expertise and knowledge) to provide optimized impact through cyclical markets and a global economy.

Learn more about clients, industries and markets and increase capabilities to help clients find better solutions, apply technological advancements, and meet changing market conditions.

Use and improve knowledge to refine company expertise worldwide in core competencies of engineering and constructing client facilities, and sustain world-class effectiveness and efficiency.

To address these challenges, a small, centrally managed knowledge-management team was established to develop the enabling technology, community deployment methods, and a pragmatic approach in the organizational change issues. This organization, composed entirely of Fluor employees, collaborated with consultants to develop the vision, strategy, structure, competencies and work practices necessary to establish and successfully sustain knowledge management across the corporation, long-term.

The result of this collaboration is a knowledge-management (KM) capability that allows Fluor to quickly form and facilitate technology-enabled knowledge communities that address critical customer and project execution issues. The web-based software solution that Fluor developed to enable knowledge management across its global employee network is called *Knowledge OnLine*^{SM} The *Knowledge OnLine* system provides an environment for community knowledge capture, discussion forums, searches, calendaring, event notification, instant messaging, knowledge categorization, knowledge searches, knowledge packaging, revision management and secure remote access. In addition, the system tracks profiles of experts around the world. Today, this method of collaboration has truly changed the culture of the company and the way it does business.

Perhaps this accomplishment is best summed up by a senior manager who exclaimed, "In my 25 years with the company, I never thought this would happen. North America collaborating with South Africa — it works similarly between North America and the Philippines, North America and New Delhi and so on. The sun truly never sets on Fluor knowledge."

LESSONS:

- Globalization brings many organizational benefits, but a globally dispersed workforce finds it more difficult to know what they know, and to know where the knowledge is. Fluor has been reaping the benefits of improved access to knowledge and the ability to share on a real-time basis for a couple of years now, although there remains potential for even greater benefits. Success stories from business units all over the world continue to reinforce the value that KM brings to the corporation, and to demonstrate the power collaboration can generate between people who have never met.

- Position knowledge-sharing as a win-win proposition — because it is! As Alan Boeckmann, Chairman and Chief Executive Officer at Fluor Corporation, states, "The individual and collective application of our unparalleled knowledge will continue to distinguish Fluor from its competitors, resulting in more opportunities for employees and greater value for our shareholders."

- Remember that the bottom-line aim of a collaborative culture is not to *get* more from people, but to create an environment where people want willingly to *give* more.

RETHINKING LIFE AND WORK AT XEROX:
How the Xerox Corporation created a more productive workforce by letting employees make the rules.

The problem at Xerox's southern customer administration center (SCAC) was management over-efficiency. Xerox had long been renowned as a family-friendly organization. But when the Ford Foundation launched a study into the idea that "family friendly" practices can also help improve business results, its researchers discovered a glitch in the works: managers at SCAC were so strict about office work schedules that the predominantly female staff of 400 was being forced to use more and more of its personal days and sick time to deal with routine family matters. The managers weren't unsympathetic to the workers' personal responsibilities, and an array of work-family benefits had been in place for years. But lack of flexibility in the face of an increasingly complex and demanding outside world was creating a "worker-unfriendly" environment without anybody realizing it or talking about it. Managers feared that if they granted more flexible working hours, productivity would decline. Workers fearing management disapproval if they asked for greater freedom were creating the "family time" they needed by other means. As a result, unplanned absences at SCAC were increasing, phone stations were being left unattended, customers were being inadequately served, growing workforce frustration was leading to an accelerated staff turnover — all of it bad for business and all of it in the name of presumed efficiency. When the researchers found similar problems at the Dallas sales/service office and the engineering unit in Webster, New York, they went back to Xerox with a novel suggestion: Why not take scheduling out of the managers' hands and let the employees deal with it themselves? The workers know what their jobs require. They also know what their lives are throwing at them. Let them sort out their own working arrangements — less-rigid hours, compressed work weeks, mutually agreed "quiet times," greater freedom to come and go as required — whatever will help to make life and work co-exist more harmoniously. These are responsible adults after all. They like the company. They're good at their jobs. The work will still get done.

Xerox agreed to try it, told management at the three centers being studied to hand work schedules over to their employees, and sat back to see what would happen. What happened is that the workforces accepted the challenge gladly, formed self-managed task forces from among their own ranks, and immediately began looking for new approaches to flexible working hours that would take everyone's needs into account. The results were striking: At SCAC, employee morale soared, staff turnover immediately declined, customers began reporting dramatically improved service, and the rate of absenteeism dropped 30 percent. In the Dallas office, sales revenues actually exceeded projections for the year, as cross-functional teams made up of front-line sales, service and support people began addressing not just their department's working hours, but questions of work/family conflicts in general, hiring practices and even staff evaluation methods. And when the office color business team at Webster engineering was given greater autonomy over its work schedule, they amazed everyone by launching the new Xerox 4700 color printer on schedule — an almost unheard-of event in an industry notorious for last-minute setbacks and delayed product launches.

The success of the Ford Foundation's "people power" experiment was so impressive that "Rethinking Life and Work" has now become a major strategy in determining how work gets done at Xerox.

LESSONS:

- If workforce attitudes and behavior are becoming counter-productive, look first at management practices. Nine times out of 10, that is where the obstacle to productivity will be found.
- Even if the workforce isn't complaining openly, remember that outmoded company rules in a rapidly changing environment can produce hidden resentments. Review the rules regularly and talk about them with the people they apply to.
- Encourage front-line employees to discuss all work place problems candidly and without fear of punishment. The obstacles they're confronting every day may be ones you've never even thought of.

- Look for ways to give employees greater decision-making authority over the material circumstances of their working lives. Nothing stifles collaborative initiative like the sense of resignation that comes from feeling powerless. Nothing encourages it more than letting people know they are trusted.

ALIXPARTNERS REDEFINES TRAINING:
How a corporate turnaround consulting firm used collaboration and knowledge-sharing to create a solid solution for training staff in a core competency area.

AlixPartners is a corporate performance improvement and turn-around consulting firm that solves complex financial, operational, transactional and litigation challenges for companies. The firm was looking for a more consistent and efficient approach to developing competency in one of its core business processes:

When the AlixPartners staff arrives at a distressed or bankrupt company, there is great urgency to find out where the cash inflows are coming from and where the outflows are going. This process requires building a 13-week liquidity (or cash) model to approximate the ebb and flow of cash, and particularly to identify when cash might run out. The model is used to help the company's management team control cash flow on a day-to-day basis in keeping with a "cash is king" mantra.

Building this critical tool takes a specific set of not-so-common skills and knowledge. The original solution to meeting this need was to hire an external consultant (Julie Kowalski of Creative Partnerships, Inc.) to develop a training program based on what other organizations had done to teach financial modeling. But in trying to gain a better understanding of what it would take to pass on the necessary skill and knowledge, Kowalski soon discovered that a generic version of traditional training would never be effective in this situation. For one thing, the process for building a cash model in the "combat" conditions created by bankruptcy was most successfully mastered through direct experience.

Beyond the glaring need for a training solution sat a more subtle need. AlixPartners had developed best practices that helped establish the firm as a leader in its industry, yet did not have a formal system for passing on its "mastery." As the value of the intellectual capital around cash modeling became more apparent, the firm was eager to use it more strategically to provide more value to its clients.

It soon became obvious that the firm needed a non-traditional solution — for several reasons:

AlixPartners consultants were so bright and highly educated, that traditional classroom training tended to bore them.

The expertise needed to develop any credible development tool had to come from seasoned modelers, yet these "experts" were not trainers and were already committed to building models on existing engagements.

Specific skills and knowledge varied greatly from consultant to consultant. Starting everyone at the same level would have created significant gaps for some and overlaps for others.

AlixPartners was, naturally, very sensitive to the perception that consultants were being trained on the client's "clock." The firm needed to find a way to bring people up to speed quickly, effectively and in a client-friendly manner.

Switching from classroom training to "something else" also changed the project requirements. A project that had seemed simple enough to outsource had transitioned into a complex collaborative experience involving numerous internal staff. In a world where the consultants were already working at 110-percent capacity, the bar for project success had just been raised significantly. Nonetheless, requests for support went out to the field and soon a team of individuals from a variety of levels and positions was created to provide subject matter expertise throughout the project.

These subject-matter experts determined that the most effective approach to meeting the learners' needs would be a simulation. The simulation required developing a fictitious company and creating a "live" engagement through which learners could get the direct experience they needed to begin mastery of the skills.

A team of consultants with a broad range of different experiences worked together to reverse-engineer the financial documents for the fictitious company. This was a time-consuming and complex task that no one in the organization had ever attempted before. Pulling it off required a huge amount of effort, personal commitment and coordination on the part of the numerous subject-matter experts.

Further down the line, the technology and training groups got involved in building an intranet for the simulation. The intranet would be used to make the simulation more realistic. Participants would use it to communicate with various company "managers" to gain information they needed to build their model. Throughout the simulation, they would also get outbound emails from the "managers" that created the same type of chaos experienced in a real engagement.

When the program actually runs, it is, of course, an exercise in which people learn through simulated experience. This provides the hands-on experience necessary for mastery of the basic skills such as information gathering, data analysis, client management and building the model using Excel. The second goal of passing on best practices of AlixPartners' most seasoned modelers is accomplished through the mentors who work one-on-one with the learners to guide them through individual learning challenges. But the learning doesn't stop there. Because the mentors have a unique set of experiences, perspectives and expertise, they are able to multiply their own intellectual capital by sharing with each other as they solve the problems that surface across the modeling teams.

The outcome of this collaborative effort is an overwhelming success. AlixPartners has a high-impact program that justifies pulling consultants at high billing rates off the job to learn. The successful design and implementation of the financial modeling simulation contribute to increasing the intellectual capital of the firm and perpetuation of the firm's reputation for exceptional expertise and client service.

The simulation is just as successful from a participant's point of view. Some participants come in having never even attempted a cash model before — and by the end of the session they've actually built one! In fact, prospective participants think so highly of the training that there is a waiting list for future sessions. Most telling, from a human perspective, is that every time the session is run, participants ask: "How do I get to be a role-player?" "How can I become a mentor?" "How can I stay involved in this?"

LESSONS:

- Rather than trying to start the learning at the midpoint of learner readiness, use online tools so that people can access what they need — when they need it. Specific skills and knowledge will always vary greatly from participant to participant. Traditional training approaches start everyone at the same level — which creates gaps and overlaps.   AlixPartners built knowledge-share documents and posted them on the mock intranet. Through this system, individuals could obtain content on specific topics to supplement their current knowledge.

- Give people the technical framework and allow them to decide how they want to apply that framework to make good decisions. There is no one "right way" for everyone. AlixPartners found there was no one thing that makes people great modelers. That means there is no magic formula to teach. Everyone has different biases and approaches — and they can all be successful. Equip people and then allow them to create their own success stories.

- Reinforce the fact that in creative collaboration, people learn from each other. Participants gain much from the wisdom and experience of mentors — as well as from their team members. But mentors learn too. The experienced financial modelers learn to translate what they experience as "second nature" so that someone else can utilize it. As they assist participants in the simulation, mentors learn how to ask questions, how to really listen and become better at mentoring. They also collaborate with one another to find alternative ways to approach an issue or solve a problem.

- Someone needs to "champion" the project. At AlixPartners, Lori Wathen, director of Organizational Development and Human Resources, worked to gain and sustain organizational support for the project. The simulation model was new to the organization, and not easily understood nor quickly embraced. As well, the development process was long and resource-intensive. Despite all this, Walthen made sure that the process stayed on track, negotiated for needed resources and cleared barriers that surfaced along the way.

- If you are already using simulation, add a knowledge-sharing component. The way to get quick results from training is with this powerful combination. In the AlixPartners example, knowledge was shared by mentor interactions, documents on the intranet, and planned "interruptions" during the training, in which participants are asked to discuss: "Based on what we've just experienced, what have we learned about what to do or not to do?"

COLLABORATING ON ROLES AND RESPONSIBILITIES:
How corporate and field leadership at Adelphia
co-created a more decentralized organization.

Adelphia Communications is one of the nation's leading cable companies with more than 5.3 million residential customers nationwide. In June 2002, Adelphia filed for bankruptcy, and in January 2003, Bill Schleyer (chairman and chief executive officer) and Ron Cooper (chief operating officer) were brought in.

The company had been very centralized, and the new leadership believed that rather than one national organization, Adelphia was really interacting with customers, competitors, franchising authorities, suppliers, and employees at a local level. In order to be successful in that model, the organization needed to be highly decentralized, and have resources and authority distributed throughout.

To shift more decision-making responsibility to managers in the field, a new level of field staff (vice president) was created in the five regions. Next came the job of deciding which responsibilities would be covered at the corporate level and which by the regions. In order to map these roles and responsibilities, a series of facilitated discussions were held across the company. Each of the senior leaders who had responsibility for a functional area (Human Resources, Law and Government Affairs, Marketing, Engineering, and Finance) put together a group of people from both corporate staff and field staff for a collaborative two-day event to bring to life the ways in which they would contribute to the mission, values, strategy and operating model for the business.

In Human Resources, for example, the head of HR collaborated with three corporate HR VPs and the five HR VPs from the field. This team created its own mission to directly reflect the business mission, they took the organization's values and translated them specifically to behaviors that all HR leaders agreed to demonstrate, and they created high-level HR objectives that tied into the strategic business imperatives. Finally, they agreed on an operating model that was tied to the concept of collaboration: The regions were empowered to identify, decide and solve their problems, and corporate was to support them with expert advice, help and counsel. It was corporate's additional responsibility to stay on top of trends that needed to be translated for enterprise-wide solutions.

LESSONS:

- Clarifying roles and responsibilities is really important, but creating a collaborative partnership, and looking out for one another, are just as crucial. At Adelphia, the phrase that the HR community uses is "we've got each other's back."
- Roles and responsibilities will overlap. David Brunick, senior vice president of Human Resources at Adelphia: "I like to use the example of a paycheck. In a lot of environments (and in Adelphia's when I arrived) there is so much finger-pointing between corporate and the field about why a paycheck was wrong. My view is we all play a role in making paychecks arrive on time and be right, and if a paycheck is late or wrong, we have failed as an HR community, and we need to figure out together how we're going to fix that."
- Collaboration does not (and should not!) eliminate conflict. Brunick again: "Collaboration does not necessarily mean affiliation. At Adelphia, collaboration means taking every difficult possible roadblock to success and throwing it out in the room and asking people to check their egos and start to work on them even though it's about giving up turf and territory. So all of these meetings, although highly collaborative, had plenty of conflict. And that's okay. I think effective collaboration demands conflict."

VITESSE GOT PEOPLE ON THE SAME PAGE:
How universal access to information
made everybody's job easier.

Two years ago, when Jennifer Reed was hired by Vitesse as the director of Marketing Communications, one of her pressing challenges was to find the data that her department needed in order to do its job. Vitesse is a leading designer and manufacturer of innovative silicon solutions and optical devices used in the networking, communications and storage industries worldwide. At a certain point in the development of Vitesse's new products, marketers needed to start developing product launch plans, but important product-related information (lead times for manufacturing, when customers will be sampled, etc.) couldn't be located, or couldn't be found in time. The business consequence was that divisions wanted products launched and the marketing communications department wasn't in a position to support them.

At the core of this problem was the fact that there were no central databases where marketing people could get timely, reliable information. Everybody was keeping their own private databases on their hard drives or in Excel spreadsheets. Which meant that there were many owners and gatekeepers to various pieces of crucial information, but no company-wide facilitators. Another area of concern was that much of the information was incorrect. There was no collaboration, no system of cross-checking, and no accountability or responsibility for making sure any of the data was valid.

As Reed began looking at how to solve this problem for her group, she discovered that many groups in the company, especially those on the operations side, were facing the same issues. So she formed a task force of 11 representatives of different groups in the company to identify the key issues, and then to look at ways to resolve the situation. Here's how the team saw the overall problem: When people throughout the organization needed information, they either didn't know where to get it, how to get it or how to access it in a timely manner. The solution was to create a universal database of single-sourced information (not repeated in multiple databases) for the company to access.

The collaborative tool currently has a host of applications that store various kinds of crucial data — from pricing, waivers and non-disclosure agreements, to a product master that houses product specifications and development status for any Vitesse product. Today employees can quickly access reports and query for specific information. The result is a knowledge-sharing system that makes everyone's job easier.

LESSONS:

- Remember that people will react to new initiatives in predictable ways. What seemed an obvious solution to an outsider was not so obvious to those on the inside who were comfortable in the old environment. Initially, Vitesse employees resisted the change. They were afraid that "new" meant "hard" and "more work." And one of the biggest challenges the task force faced was in convincing people to relinquish control — to stop building their own private repositories of information, and to risk putting their information in a central place for everyone to access.

- Remember, too, that people embrace change when they are shown what the advantages are for them personally. To counter the "This is how we have always done it" syndrome, the task force verbally walked employees through their work processes, asking questions along the way that included "How are you checking your data for accuracy? Wouldn't you prefer to access information for your report immediately rather than tracking it down?" and "What happens if you act on bad data?"

- When working on technology issues, collaborate with your technical talent. The realization that Vitesse had a major problem with information accessing occurred simultaneously to the director of Marketing Communication and to two database developers, so they decided to work together to find a solution. A key member of the task force was the IT professional who was building Vitesse's customer relationship management (CRM) tool. He was already in the process of creating a tool for the sales team that expanded to become the model for the universal database.

- Keep things simple at the start. The task force decided to focus on just a couple of applications that were fairly simple and that asked only small groups to input data. This way they could work one-on-one with individuals to build their buy-in and to ensure proper development of procedures. They began with the sales team, because the vice president of Sales and Marketing was already committed to the CRM and knew that his group was being badly affected by a lack of information for reporting and forecasts. Thus he was receptive to the idea that centralized information could be the solution. Success in this department also gave high visibility (and credibility) to the project.

THE GREAT GAME OF BUSINESS:
How Jack Stack broke down the information barrier at International Harvester by treating employees like business partners.

When Jack Stack arrived at International Harvester's factory in Springfield, Missouri, the engine remanufacturing plant was losing $2 million a year on revenues of $26 million. Stack and the 119 employees of the now independent Springfield Remanufacturing Corporation initiated an amazing turnaround. Ten years after he bought the company, SRC had sales of $73 million and the firm hired almost 600 additional workers. How did he do that? By making information available. Stack created a system called "The Great Game of Business," which was designed to teach every employee about the entire business — including the finances of the company. The goal was to give people inside the organization as much information as companies give shareholders every quarter. Each Wednesday employees got a complete analysis of the entire company — income statement, balance sheet and cash flow for the month. As workers came to understand the entire picture, they also learned how their jobs fit into the whole. So successful was Stack's "The Great Game of Business," that SRC now schools other corporations in the rules of the game.

Information is the nutrient of all living systems. In any organization, how information is handled determines whether it is an obstacle to or a liberator of creative collaboration. In traditional management structures, restricting access to information or doling it out on a "need-to-know" basis decreases employees' power. At SRC, information is used to include and empower the workforce. The incredible turnaround at SRC could not have happened without Stack's involving every worker through increased access to information — and then investing heavily in the education and personal development of employees so that they would have enough basic background to utilize the business data he shared.

Stack started his corporate transformation with small steps. When he first took over management of the International Harvester division, his primary goal was to increase productivity. Each day he gave foremen the results of how well their people did the day before — how many units they had produced and what percentage of those units contained defects. He also gave them productivity scores for their particular department compared with the other departments within the plant as a whole, so that all five foremen knew how they stood individually and as a group. The first time the division broke its previous productivity record, Stack gathered the foremen and bought them a round of coffee and let them take time to talk, laugh and feel good about their accomplishment. The second time they broke the record, he bought coffee *and* donuts. The third time, he invited the foremen to his house for pizza and poker.

LESSONS:

- Think of yourself and your workforce as equally intelligent partners in a war of ideas against the competition. Business literacy coupled with trust triggers inspiration. Give your employees all the information you can and trust they'll come up with the answers you need. If they don't, you haven't lost anything. If they *can't,* you may have.
- When large-scale change is required in an organization, cushion the impact by breaking the process down into individual steps that everyone can understand and deal with. Celebrate each small victory along the way. Be generous with congratulations, but don't be patronizing about it. Your workforce isn't made up of good boys and girls. It's made up of thoughtful, intelligent men and women. They know the difference between being taken for a ride and being invited on board.

COLLABORATIVE PROBLEM RESOLUTION:
How Cisco Systems created a communication
strategy to address critical business issues.

Cisco Systems, Inc. is a global leader in networking for the Internet, employing a workforce of more than 34,000. Cisco's Internet Protocol-based (IP) networking solutions are the foundation of the Internet and many corporate, education and government networks around the world. Like many companies, Cisco is continually seeking new ways to address its key business challenges. Being a large, global organization, cross-functional problems tend to be the hardest to handle, yet resolving them generally yields the greatest benefits in terms of improved productivity.

In 2002, the sales management of Cisco set out to establish an effective method of tackling cross-functional business issues. Management believed that the key to addressing these issues lay in establishing a communication process that would enable employees from across the company to share knowledge, brainstorm issues, recommend decisions to senior management and implement solutions quickly and efficiently. With this in mind, a global team was set up to develop a Collaborative Problem Resolution (CPR) process.

Despite the best intentions, getting a random group of people to share information and make strategic business decisions rarely results in aligned action. Lengthy daily meetings also cost the company time and money. CPR seeks to address this by providing a methodology that brings the right people together and helps them prioritize and focus on critical issues. The team works under the guidance of a skilled facilitator, a team leader, and an executive sponsor whose key role is to ensure that decisions are made and acted upon.

The initial CPR process was designed by a team working in Cisco's Europe, Middle East and Africa (EMEA) operation. Senior leadership identified their top business challenges, and a team was brought together to identify solutions. Based on the work done in EMEA, a global cross-functional team was created to build a similar methodology.

The global team came together to test the process that would ultimately be established as CPR. According to Ayelet Baron, senior manager, Worldwide Sales Strategy, "We defined our business issue as: We have an inconsistent global methodology to identify, prioritize and address complex business problems, resulting in inefficiency, productivity loss, lack of cross-functional communication and issues not getting resolved." This presented the opportunity to establish a methodology to solve these complex business issues in a short space of time.

The CPR methodology was put to the test in Cisco's Asia Pacific operation, where senior leadership was keen to verticalize the sales force by shifting the customer focus onto key industries such as banking, retail, healthcare and public sector. An executive sponsor invited members to join a cross-functional team of colleagues from Cisco's EMEA and US operations, and corporate headquarters. The two-day session was held in Singapore and involved 20 participants. Day one began with some interactive exercises designed to help team members get to know each other. The team leader, from the Asia Pacific operation, provided some background to the business problem and team members from the EMEA and US operations shared their best practices around the subject. The rest of the day was spent defining exactly what were the issues that verticalization would address in that region.

On day two, the team split into three groups. The first group focused on defining the organizational structure and coming up with key action plans. The second group created a channel strategy, and the third group worked on specific programs and initiatives around the issue, including marketing and communication strategies. The team then regrouped to review and revise their work, and draw up a business plan. This was presented to senior management the following week, and approved immediately. The recommended business plan has now been implemented in the Asia Pacific operation, and the team will continue to track the measurable objectives. This entire CPR process took only one month from design to implementation.

The success of CPR can be measured in many ways. Nitin Kawale, the senior director of Worldwide Sales Strategy, sees the key benefit to Cisco as the ability to systemically address cross-functional issues. "We now, in essence, have a game plan to tackle issues that will yield the greatest increase in productivity. " But Phil Smith, senior director of EMEA sales operations, states it another way: "When pulling together a CPR team, make sure this is driven and supported from the top and believed in from the bottom. If you get CPR right you could find a way of unlocking magic that is in all of our organizations, but is sometimes clouded by our organizational structures."

LESSONS:

- Devise and develop processes that spread knowledge and inquiry throughout the various functions of an organization. A critical success factor of the CPR process is its ability to help teams focus on key business issues faced by the organization, by increasing internal communication across functions.
- In any problem-solving session, don't let your team jump into recommendations and solutions before they've defined the problem. The CPR team spends its first session defining the business problem and establishing common terms of reference. During this time, the facilitator's job is to keep participants focused on agreeing what the business problem is, before moving on to possible resolutions.
- It's (always!) the people. Having the right people on the CPR team is critical to its success. Members must bring some element of expertise to the meetings, should already have a grasp of the business challenge in question and come prepared with ideas for possible solutions.
- Remember that collaborative processes require "soft skill" competencies. Facilitation, listening, building trust, creating a vision and common objective — all are crucial to the success of CPR. And for many professionals, these will be new ways of behaving and thinking.

WHO IS THAT GUY AT THE BACK OF THE ROOM?
How Bob Buckman reinforced a
knowledge-sharing culture based on trust.

Buckman Laboratories has been in the specialty chemical business since 1945. Under the leadership of Robert H. (Bob) Buckman, it also became a world-class, networked, knowledge-sharing organization. Buckman Labs has 1,400 associates (their word for employees) and customers in 80 countries.

At every knowledge-management conference that I've ever attended or addressed, Bob has been quoted, and Buckman Labs has been held up as a "best practice" example. Anyone who wants to know how to create and lead a "new model" company should read Bob's book, *Building a Knowledge Driven Organization,* for the inside story from the man who led the charge.

Bob would tell you that converting a command-and-control organization into a networked one was not without its challenges and setbacks. Still, by 1994, Buckman Labs had jumped into full-bore knowledge-sharing: new software and connectivity had been installed, most of the associates were equipped with laptops, and online Forums were up and running. To honor and reward the top 150 people from around the world (regardless of title or function) who had done the best job of sharing knowledge with the new technologies, a "Fourth Wave Meeting" was held in Scottsdale, Arizona. The meeting was three days of fun, celebration and work — specifically, critical discussions about business trends and strategies. It was also the setting for the following story:

Through the entire conference, a man wearing shorts, a T-shirt, and sandals sat at the back of the room, chronicling the meeting on his laptop and sending live messages onto the Forum for the rest of the company to read. His name was Mark Koskiniemi. About midway through the meeting, one of the organizers (a manager) approached Mark and asked him to stop sending out notes on the meeting. Mark refused by saying he didn't feel that was appropriate. When the organizer suggested that the request to cease came from the top, Mark countered by saying he'd appreciate hearing it personally.

A few minutes later, a break was called, and Mark found himself face-to-face with Bob Buckman. Here is how Mark recalls the conversation:

Mark: Hello, sir.

Bob: Mark, I understand that you have been posting notes from the meeting on the Forum. I have to say that I have not read them, but are you sure that is such a good idea?

Mark: Do you trust me?

Bob broke into a big smile, nodded slightly, and nothing further was said about Mark's continued reporting of the events.

There were two results from Koskiniemi's reporting:

1. In all, he sent more than 50 Forum or e-mail messages related to the reports coming from the meeting, and there was a lot of interest on the part of those not in attendance to know what was happening. Buckman associates who weren't there really appreciated being kept in the loop.
2. The higher the level of trust between an organization and its employees, the more knowledge-sharing will take place. Koskiniemi (who is now head of Buckman's operation in Australia and New Zealand) experienced the power of that reality: "If knowledge-sharing is built on trust, then to me this moment over any other demonstrated that Bob Buckman really trusted the associates of Buckman Laboratories to take the company forward."

LESSONS:
- Trust is the foundation for knowledge-sharing. It is the conduit through which knowledge flows. Without trust,

an organization loses its emotional "glue." In a culture of suspicion people withhold information, hide behind psychological walls, withdraw from participation. If you want to create a networked organization, the first and most crucial step is to build a culture of trust.

- I've said it before, but it bears repeating: Trust is a two-way street. Leaders must be trusted — but they also must trust. Encouraging workforce participation and responsibility requires a deep belief in the potential of your employees to make responsible decisions. And to prepare for making responsible decisions, people must be entrusted with information, resources, support, encouragement, responsibility, and authority.

- Values-in-action begins with values-based leadership. As Lura Powell said: "The challenge is to make sure that values aren't just words you post on the website, but are really the principles you live by. People are watching. If corporate officers don't adhere to the values, and use them as an important part of the road map moving forward, everyone knows it — and the whole thing falls apart."

BECOMING A LEARNING ORGANIZATION:
How After Action Reviews drive knowledge-sharing and innovation at J.M. Huber Corporation.

May 2, 2003 at the J.M. Huber Corporation headquarters in Edison, New Jersey, was marked by a special occasion — the Breakfast of Champions and the presentation of the Chairman's Award for After Action Review (AAR) Excellence. That morning, Board Chair, President and Chief Executive Officer Peter Francis handed the coveted award, a handsome glass globe and engraved plaque, to the cross-functional team that had earned it.

The four-member team had worked diligently to develop and implement an enterprise risk-management program. Integral to that project was the selection of a software vendor that could supply risk management services designed to record, measure and report various types of financial exposures across Huber's diverse businesses, which include oil and gas exploration and drilling, mining, manufacturing, timberlands management and financial services.

When Francis presented the award to the deserving team, he remarked: "I selected this team because they fully integrated the AAR process into their project plan, using AARs to implement a critically important system on time, within budget, and with an exceptional level of quality. The team avoided 'recreating the wheel' by applying lessons learned from other teams. They also contributed to Huber's knowledge base by providing new lessons learned that others at Huber can apply in the future."

AARs? What are they? And why are they so vitally important to this successful, multinational, privately held company?

The After Action Review (AAR) was developed by the United States Army during the 1970s, at a time when W. Edwards Deming's pioneering work on Total Quality Management was beginning to be adopted by Japanese and American corporations. The AAR process helped American soldiers learn from their mistakes and from their correct judgement — with the intention of preventing future errors, continuing successful activities and finding new solutions to problems.

Basically, the AAR process assembles people who were involved in a planned project or an unscheduled event and asks them to answer three questions:

1. What happened?
2. Why did it happen?
3. What should we do about it?

By using a disciplined approach to problem-solving, the people are asked to analyze the situation dispassionately. They identify what worked so that the actions can be repeated for future success; they note what didn't work so problems can be prevented.

In 1996, the AAR process came to the attention of Peter Francis. He believed that if the J.M. Huber Corporation could establish its own AAR process, it would give employees around the world the chance to capture knowledge and share it effectively. Francis led the effort to create a process the entire company could use, and he sought the assistance of Pete Tortorello, vice president of Enabling Technologies. Tortorello leads four key functions — Human Resources, Information Technology, Corporate Communications and Learning Technologies — all critical to the successful development and implementation of the AAR process.

"From the beginning, we were excited about the learning we could achieve through AARs," Francis said, "but there were no ready-made tools to implement the process. That's when we decided to make our own."

Huber created its own half-hour training videotape that walks employees through a typical AAR meeting, showing all aspects of the AAR in action. The company also published a guidebook and offers facilitator training. "The AAR video and other training materials are used in all our new hire orientations," said Tortorello. "From the moment they begin their careers at Huber, our employees are exposed to AARs as an important learning tool, and they are equipped with the skills they need to participate in AARs."

Central to the process is a sophisticated database that captures, stores, reminds and reports on accumulated learning. Employees can access the AAR tools directly from the AAR web site on the company's intranet.

To conduct an AAR, employees can download an information-gathering template that also helps to guide the face-to-face discussions that are the basis of the AAR. After employees answer the three basic questions, they can input their learning and post it immediately to the database. Other employees around the world can search the database to find AARs on topics related to their work. The AARs are rich with facts, experiences, advice and lessons learned.

The AAR database also has unique interactive features that make it truly helpful. It allows employees to subscribe to AARs on topics of interest to them. Each week, newly submitted AARs on the selected topics are e-mailed to individual employees who request them. In addition, the system sends e-mailed reminder notices to employees who have participated in the AAR process and committed to action items that must be completed by a specified time. Huber's AAR web site also includes online training modules, downloadable guidebooks and instructional videotapes.

"Our fundamental aim is to build a learning habit," Francis said.

It's not surprising. One of the company's stated principles is learning. Huber's vision for itself and its employees is that they will "grow profitably, both personally and as a company, through the discovery and application of knowledge."

In just a few years, Huber transformed itself from a company that was just starting its own AAR process from scratch to one that is embedding it solidly into the culture. In 2002, Huber employees conducted more than 2,000 AARs — against a goal of 1,000 for the year. As the number of AARs has steadily increased over the years, the quality and value of the AARs have improved, too. Huber employees completed over 90 percent of the action items they committed to in their 2002 AARs — greater than the stated target. Now more than half of all AARs conducted focus on the company's Critical Success Factors, aligning learning with areas of strategic importance to the company.

"The AAR process is a key component of Huber's approach to becoming a learning organization," said Tortorello. "Of course, conducting AARs is not just about reaching some magic number. It is about applying knowledge and sharing lessons learned with each other. Ultimately, this learning tool helps us repeat our successes, avoid past mistakes and improve performance."

There are two main reasons for the success of AARs at Huber. First, it has the unwavering support of the chairman and his management team. Messages from Francis reiterate the AAR goals and significance to the company. Periodic updates keep employees informed about their progress toward the yearly goals. And, Francis sponsors the annual Chairman's Award for After Action Review Excellence. Second, the AAR process is convenient and easy to use. Huber intentionally built it that way. Because the AAR process is available online, the majority of employees always have the tools within fingertips' reach.

"Completing an AAR is like making project notes for yourself and for others," said Tortorello. "AARs make it possible to track action items that relate to a project implementation or process. It's a way to take a 'to do' list one step further. It is an additional benefit to be able to use the AAR online research library. Based on your own specifications, it pushes information to you."

The award-winning Enterprise Risk Management team honored in May was able to apply the lessons learned from the work of Huber project teams that had gone before them, which already had been captured in previous AARs. The team uncovered and applied several key strategies offered in their colleagues' AARs that helped them not only select the best vendor for the job, but also allowed them to make important contributions to the company.

For example, they instituted an internal audit process, included contingency factors in their capital appropriations request, learned about the vendor's business model, negotiated a favorable contract and kept costs within budget.

"The Enterprise Risk Management team is exemplary in its use of AARs," said Tortorello. "This team hit on all cylinders, using all the AAR resources to their fullest extent, from searching the database and subscribing to AARs to contributing their own AARs back into the pool of knowledge."

Huber's commitment to learning extends beyond its own walls. Other businesses that benefited from the successful results of Huber's AAR process have asked to participate in AAR discussions. One of Huber's major customers — a consumer goods manufacturer whose brands are household names — asked Huber to assist its employees in establishing their own AAR processes. Huber eagerly jumped in to help.

According to Tortorello, the AAR process can only flourish and make a genuine difference when it is supported by a corporate culture where people feel safe in candid discussions; where they won't be chastised for making mistakes; and where the senior leaders promote and model the healthy dialogue that AARs are meant to generate and document. "The AAR process works at Huber because our leaders from the chairman on reinforce a learning culture and operate according to principles that honor the integrity and dignity of every person and encourage innovation from every employee," Tortorello said.

In fact, the three basic questions that are asked during the AAR process reinforce the company's inclination for learning. The question "What happened?" leads to honest self evaluation. The question "Why did it happen?" provides an opportunity for analytical problem solving. And the last question, "What should we do about it?" promotes a bias toward action.

"AARs are helping us build the kind of culture we want to thrive at Huber," said Francis.

Even though Huber has a database full of great ideas and information, nobody at the company thinks they have all the answers. At the annual Breakfast of Champions, Francis made that clear when he said: "We're on a journey toward becoming a learning organization. It's a continuing process, not a destination point. At

Huber, we've realized that learning and growth and profitability are inexorably linked. We just facilitate the connections by giving our employees the tools. They deserve the credit for using them to the best of their ability — and for striving always to do a better job."

LESSONS:

- Create an environment for learning with the following key elements: demonstrated support from senior leadership; a safe environment for honest self-evaluation; a standard, consistent process that is easily accessible, convenient and useful for all employees; ongoing communication and training to reinforce the learning message.
- Build a learning habit. Establish concrete goals — such as the number and quality of AARs completed each year. Provide tips on how to reach those goals. Track progress and announce periodic milestones to all employees.
- Recognize and reward employees for contributing to the shared learning. Give an annual Chairman's award; communicate success stories broadly throughout the organization to show employees what effective learning is and how it is accomplished. Expect leaders to model the learning behavior.
- Print out and pin up on your wall the following statement from W. Edwards Deming: *"Learning is not compulsory ... neither is survival."*

EMPLOYEE COMMUNICATIONS IN THE PIAZZA:
How Caterpillar created an environment in which employees from many different backgrounds and cultures came together.

A *Fortune* 100 company, Caterpillar is the world's leading manufacturer of construction and mining equipment, diesel and natural gas engines and industrial gas turbines. The company is a technology leader in construction, transportation, mining, forestry, energy, logistics, electronics, financing and electric power generation.

Caterpillar products and components are manufactured in 50 U.S. facilities and in 65 other locations around the globe. At Caterpillar's European headquarters in Geneva, Switzerland, employees represent a mixture of nationalities from all over the world. While essential for a successful global operation, this diversity complicates communications: not only are employees dealing with multiple languages and backgrounds, they're interacting with people who come from very different communication cultures. The challenge was how to make this diverse population begin to think of themselves as a team.

A few years ago, Employee Communication Manager Gottardo Bontagnali kept thinking about the role played by the central market square — "piazza" in Italian — in virtually all European villages. In addition to going there for necessities of daily life, villagers went there to exchange news, pick up gossip, pass on information and socialize. It was, and still is in many places, the village's most efficient communications tool.

So Bontagnali decided to create a "piazza" at Caterpillar's Geneva headquarters, based on the village theme. Local artists were brought in to paint the walls of the top-floor cafeteria with large village scenes — dotted with bright yellow Cat machines, of course — as well as sights from multiple Cat locations. And the villagers portrayed in the panoramas were actual Cat employees. The result was amazing: with a little imagination, you could actually picture yourself in a European market square surrounded by familiar faces and sights.

Employees were then encouraged to use the "piazza" for informal meetings and discussions. "Let's discuss it over a cup of coffee in the Piazza" has now become part of the Caterpillar's business culture in Geneva. And because so many people use it for regular exchanges, it's become an important means of sharing information on an impromptu basis as well. But the most impressive result is how workplace design helped build workforce camaraderie and a common sense of purpose. Caterpillar's Piazza is a wonderful example of taking a time-honored local tradition and using it to address a modern business challenge.

LESSONS:

- Look at how your workplace layout encourages or impedes the way the organization communicates. To facilitate communication and knowledge-sharing, you need to create social environments that stimulate both arranged and chance conversations. Attractive break-out areas, coffee bars, comfortable cafeteria chairs, even wide landings on staircases — all of these increase the likelihood that employees will encounter one another and linger to talk.

- Design your culture and your organization to encourage serendipity. IDEO's studios in Palo Alto, California, are laid out so that everyone sees and hears everyone else's design problems. One day two of IDEOs engineers were designing a device for an electric razor to vacuum up cut hair. They were meeting at a table in front of another engineer's workstation, who soon joined the discussion by saying that he'd once worked on a similar problem for a completely different application. He ended up bringing out samples and a report he'd written.

- Meeting for coffee in the Piazza worked for Caterpillar, and something like it could work for your organization as well. PARC Xerox added a technology element, and brought people together by wiring the coffeepot to the internet. Any time that someone brewed a fresh pot of coffee, a signal went up on the net. People would come out of their offices from various parts of the building for a cup, and they would all meet in front of the coffeepot. As a next step, Xerox installed huge white boards around the coffee area, so that people could actually start a conversation and write out key points. This, in turn, allowed others who were in the area to see where the discussion was heading, and to also join in.

- Working in isolation can cause people to lose the sense of belonging to a group. When Bill Beddow, manager of Corporate Communications and Corporate Public Affairs, first told me this Caterpillar story, he said it reminded him of a particular episode in his favorite TV show, *Northern Exposure:* "In the small town of Cicely, Alaska, the local laundromat played the same role as the European piazza. One of the characters, Maggie, buys a home washer/dryer for convenience, but little by little realizes that the technology has cut her off from one of the most important social conventions of Cicely life. So she eventually returns the appliances and resumes her 'inconvenient' weekly treks to the village coin laundry. It was the most wonderful and unforgettable episode!"

THE MORAL OF THE STORIES

With one exception, success in today's global economy boils down to the single, universally recognized objective of getting more for less. The exception is human resource. The potential of an organization lies within each individual and within the connections between individuals. Human labor is no longer a disposable commodity. It is a unique creative resource for the future of the organization. You can trim production costs, speed up communications, reduce delivery times, even cut corners on marketing and promotion — but you can't devalue workers and expect to come out ahead. If you give people less, they give less back. If you treat them like underlings, they behave like underlings. Offer them more, on the other hand, and they repay you with interest. I'm not talking about money now. I'm talking about liberating untapped potential, about energizing employees and engaging their commitment and enthusiasm.

Give people a chance to grow and they will blossom. Entrust them with greater authority and they will take on greater responsibility. Educate them to understand the changing business dynamics and they will make excellent business decisions. Encourage them to collaborate, and they will amaze you with their inventiveness. Treat them like full partners in the organization and they will participate like owners. Make human potential *the* corporate strategy and your company will be ready for the new business age.

This, ultimately, is the moral of all the success stories I tell at conferences and company meetings. It's a moral that today's most effective leaders have learned through experience, and one which can be put to use in any company with the application of a few leadership strategies …

HOW TO LEAD IN A BUSINESS TURNED UPSIDE DOWN

EXAMINE CHANGING REALITIES
- Help employees understand the forces of change affecting markets, competition and their jobs
- Acknowledge the changing needs and values of the workforce

ADOPT THE NEW BUSINESS MODEL
- Identify the new reality and organizational model
- Exploit instability as the opportunity for positive transformation

DEVELOP A CHANGE-ADEPT WORKFORCE

- Expand employees' skills to help them thrive on change instead of fearing it
- Develop management practices that promote change-adeptness throughout the organization

LEAD DISCONTINUOUS CHANGE

- Make sure you are asking the right questions
- Build emotional literacy into your change strategies

STRENGTHEN THE CORE OF LEADERSHIP

- Become the change you want to see in others: lead by example
- Develop leaders throughout the organization

RENEGOTIATE THE COMPACT BETWEEN EMPLOYEES AND EMPLOYERS

- Recognize the powerful potential of shared commitment
- Move from paternalism to partnerships

LIBERATE WORKFORCE POTENTIAL

- Rely on human potential as central to your corporate strategy
- Encourage, nurture, and reward creative collaboration

INDEX

Order Form

"This Isn't the Company I Joined"
How to Lead in a Business Turned Upside Down

Name:_____

Company: _____

Address:_____

City, State, Zip: _____

Phone: _____

Email: _____

KCS Bulk Discount Pricing	**U.S. Shipping & Handling**
1–24 = 20% ($23.96)	$0–$30 = $5.00
25–99 = 30% ($20.97)	$31–$60 = $6.00
100–249 = 33% ($19.95)	$61–$90 = $7.50
+250 = 35% ($19.47)	$91–$175 = $9.00
	$176+ = 5% of total

No. of copies:_____

Subtotal: _____

S & H: _____

Tax: (8.25% CA only):_____

TOTAL: _____

Send check or money order to:
Kinsey Consulting Services
P.O. Box 8255
Berkeley, CA 94707
510-526-1727

Order Form

━━━━━

"This Isn't the Company I Joined"
How to Lead in a Business Turned Upside Down

━━━━━

Name:_____

Company: _____

Address:_____

City, State, Zip: _____

Phone: _____

Email: _____

KCS Bulk Discount Pricing	U.S. Shipping & Handling	
1–24 = 20% ($23.96)	$0–$30	= $5.00
25–99 = 30% ($20.97)	$31–$60	= $6.00
100–249 = 33% ($19.95)	$61–$90	= $7.50
+250 = 35% ($19.47)	$91–$175	= $9.00
	$176+	= 5% of total

No. of copies:_____

Subtotal: _____

S & H: _____

Tax: (8.25% CA only):_____

TOTAL: _____

Send check or money order to:
Kinsey Consulting Services
P.O. Box 8255
Berkeley, CA 94707
510-526-1727